9058557

70 00
42 00

MW01517749

On the Winds and Waves of Imagination

WELLESLEY STUDIES IN CRITICAL THEORY, LITERARY HISTORY, AND CULTURE
VOLUME 20
GARLAND REFERENCE LIBRARY OF THE HUMANITIES
VOLUME 2156

Wellesley Studies in Critical Theory, Literary History, and Culture

William E. Cain, *General Editor*

On the Winds and Waves of Imagination
Transnational Feminism and Literature

Constance S. Richards

Garland Publishing, Inc.
a member of the Taylor & Francis Group
New York & London
2000

Dedicated to Ike

Published in 2000 by
Garland Publishing, Inc.
A member of the Taylor & Francis Group
29 West 35th Street
New York, NY 10001

10   9   8   7   6   5   4   3   2   1

Library of Congress Cataloging-in-Publication Data is available from
the Library of Congress

Printed on acid-free, 250-year-life paper.
Manufactured in the United States of America

Contents

v

Introduction

The following study rests upon two basic assumptions concerning the industry of literature. First, while hegemonic versions of postmodern theory may claim that the author is dead, writing literature continues to be a viable arena for the exploration of the subject, and as such, a radical act for women and for all who have been silenced. Second, this study presupposes that creating, reading, and writing about literature provide an opportunity to explore ourselves and to build alliances with others. The dialectic between the self-construction of identity and the industry of literature, that is, the acts of writing and reading, amounts to the articulation of ideology.

An adequate theory of literary criticism, therefore, must address how writers and readers situate themselves within identity categories such as the "nation" (in its various constructions), gender (and what it means in relation to power structures), and race (and what it means in relation to various power structures); such a theory must also address the diversity of experience within such categories. As readers, we bring to our reading of texts not only our own sense of who we are but also our assumptions about others; through reading literature we can explore both. Literary criticism, which acknowledges this potential in the production and consumption of literature, enables self-construction of identity and thus must be considered a political act. My study asserts that the subject positions of women in literature and the female producers of literary texts reflect the heterogeneity of women's experiences. I take a transnational feminist approach to the questions of patriarchal domination and colonial subjugation in examining postcolonial texts by women writers, focusing in particular on Virginia Woolf, who speaks from the center of empire; Zoë Wicomb, a postmodern South African subject of colonialism; and Alice Walker, who inhabits a diasporic subject position.[1] A transnational feminist approach to literature must be able to address how gender collides with race, national origin, and class in women's oppression and how women participate in and resist their own oppression and the oppression of other women. In the existing field of postcolonial literary studies, however, such analyses remain underrepresented.

Early feminist literary criticism took two forms: the identification and critical reading of "lost" literature by women writers, and the application of a feminist analysis to canonical literature, examining the situation of women within the text on the basis of gender alone. For the most part, the application of a feminist paradigm to colonial discourse seems to be at this early stage; much of it focuses solely on gender. But an examination of gender issues in colonialist and postcolonial literatures should not/cannot be seen apart from race, nation, and class. For example, in the area of "Caliban studies," Abena Busia focuses on the female characters of *The Tempest,* Miranda and Sycorax. While the "challenge for 'kingship' revolves around the prestigious exchange of virtuous European women [Miranda and her literary sisters], . . . there is no value in the traffic in native women" (91). Sycorax is missing from the text and "unvoic[ed]" in her absence (87). Busia calls attention to the centrality of bourgeois Eurocentric subjectivity, while emphasizing the fact that Sycorax represents both an exploited class and a non-European race. Stephanie Athey and Daniel Cooper Alarcón move a step further in their analysis of Aphra Behn's *Oroonoko* by contrasting the white female narrator with the African female character Imoinda, situating their critique within the context of the "three-way mediation of racial exploitation in the Americas as European peoples negotiate domination via both African and [indigenous] American populations" and the ways in which this mediation takes place on black and white female bodies (Athey and Alarcón 417). A third example is Gayatri Spivak's analysis of *Jane Eyre.* She claims that the foundational stature of this novel in Anglo-American feminist literary studies is based on an imperialist feminist reading which depends upon the Other "worlded" status of the Bertha/Antoinette character for whom Jean Rhys creates a history in *Wide Sargasso Sea.*

While these examples are evidence of a move within feminist studies toward literary interpretation that addresses the web of race, nation, class, and gender, there remains much women's literature that would benefit from being read as colonial discourse. Therefore, my strategy in chapter 1 is to examine the approaches to postcolonial studies that aim at decolonizing literature and must be considered in articulating a feminist theory of literary practice. Chapter 1 focuses in part on the centrality of Shakespeare's *The Tempest* as a master narrative of colonial discourse. Postcolonial reworkings of the play offer one method of investigating the power relations inherent in master narrative forms of literature. Transnational feminism is offered as an anticolonial approach to postcolonial literature which complicates the various constructions of nation with the issue of gender.

Toward this end, I am indebted to the editors of and contributors to the collection *Scattered Hegemonies: Postmodernity and Transnational Feminist Practices* for naming and articulating a tendency to cross boundaries which has often been present in the literature of women. As a first work exploring transnational feminism as a social strategy and theoretical practice, *Scattered Hegemonies* offers a very broad representation of transnational feminism in a variety of disciplines and fields. Kamala Visweswaran offers a critique of feminist ethnography in the form of a play. Robert Carr examines testimonials of Third World women which are produced and introduced by First World academics, raising the question of who speaks for whom. Tani Barlow employs a sociolinguistic approach to the construction of gender in modern China. Lydia Liu, Mary Layoun, and Nalini Natarajan critique specific literary texts (of China, Cyprus, and India, respectively) which employ the female body as a signifier of decolonization and nation building, yet stop short of articulating the transnational feminist potential of postcolonial literature. Norma Alarcón suggests that the feminist re-visioning of two mythic Mexican women who have historically represented the virgin-whore binary facilitates a female subject who has agency and is self-defined, yet she warns that such re-visionings can be subject to appropriation by universalist approaches to feminism which ignore how race, ethnicity, and class also determine the lived experience of real Mexican women. While these critics may not be cited specifically, many of the issues raised in these various approaches to cultural texts also emerge in my study of literature.

Of particular interest to my project are the contributors to *Scattered Hegemonies* who enable academic work across borders. Like Alarcón, both Caren Kaplan and Fred Pfeil warn against the loss of historical specificity. In arguing for a politics of location as transnational feminist practice, Kaplan prefers strategies such as Maria Lugones's concept of world traveling, which retains women's different political and historical temporalities, to homogenizing ones like Virginia Woolf's idea, articulated in *Three Guineas*, of a common world of women. Pfeil speaks to the "double shift" of theory and activism, suggesting that in both arenas a "flexible, practical relations of solidarity" is preferable to a relativist approach which values difference but does not allow for political engagement across those differences (Grewal and Kaplan 225). Inderpal Grewal compares the exploration of postmodern subjectivity in two autobiographical texts (Sara Suleri's *Meatless Days* and Gloria Anzaldúa's *Borderlands*), preferring Anzaldúa's suggestion that the decentered, postmodern self can empower an identity politics of multiplicity.

What emerges from this collection is a concept of transnational feminism that views the experience of women more broadly than do local feminisms and at the same time recognizes the limitations of a global perspective that homogenizes difference. Transnational feminism recognizes historical and political specificity and the influence of the transnational flow of capital resulting in cultural displacement, expatriation, migration, and cultural appropriation. But while Kaplan, Pfeil, and Grewal, in particular, envision a feminist theory and praxis that can cross without obliterating difference, none suggest the potential of writing and reading fiction as an arena for such a project; it is this challenge with which my work engages.

A transnational perspective seems appropriate in the aftermath of colonialism and in light of the kind of imperial power, without the benefit of colonies or former colonies, that the United States currently wields globally. Colonialism and imperialism have set in motion certain kinds of transnational interactions—movement of people, and with them national identities, ideologies, ethnicities, cultures—which are often played out in cultural production. One could say, for example, that Alice Walker's literary interaction with Africa is a product of the slave trade and of the imposition of the English language by colonial powers and settler communities. Along with the *Scattered Hegemonies* project, the writings of Chela Sandoval, María Lugones, and Arjun Appadurai have been influential in my understanding of the necessity to juggle a focus on gender with a transnational perspective and historical specificity. Their understanding of the mobility of the human spirit across boundaries of nation, geography, race, religion, and other predilections has done much in establishing a deeper and richer understanding of transnational feminist thought. Their ideas find fertile soil in my readings of Woolf, Wicomb, and Walker, but could be brought to bear as well on other contemporary women writers, such as Paule Marshall and Lorraine Hansberry, whose work also evidences a transnational feminist perspective. In advancing a transnational feminist approach to literary practice, I suggest that writers and readers in the postcolonial moment can successfully negotiate difference without effacing it.

In implementing this approach, I begin with a voice from the center of empire, not to uphold the centrality of the colonial metropole, but to illustrate a gap in colonial discourse theory that critically engages with canonical literature. For example, while Joseph Conrad's *Heart of Darkness* (1899) has been subjected to many postcolonial readings, Virginia Woolf's first novel, *The Voyage Out* (1920), which also presents a protagonist who attempts to define herself through a voyage to a Third World country, seems, for the most part, to have escaped such an analysis. Hence, chapter 2 is devoted to a rigorous interrogation of the colonial project inscribed in the works of Virginia Woolf, and to an analysis of her self-reflexive critique of identity construction in colonialist literature.

Chapter 3 explores my own approach to South African author Zoë Wicomb's novel *You Can't Get Lost in Cape Town,* using a transnational feminist reading practice called for by the strong sense of "otherness" evoked in my first read of the novel.

Chapter 4 suggests that Alice Walker's *The Color Purple, The Temple of My Familiar,* and *Possessing the Secret of Joy* construct race and gender as transnational identities, and criticize the violence perpetrated upon these aspects of identity and played out on the bodies of women by the colonial process with the collusion of indigenous patriarchy. These three novels form the foundation of my analysis of Walker as a literary practitioner of transnational feminism. As an African American, Walker is located by her displaced heritage as an "outsider" within the United States; she reinvents her African heritage based on shared race, gender, and ancestry when she chooses the imposition of traditional practices on continental African women's bodies as a site of struggle, and when she deploys her diasporic imagination in the construction of continental African women's experiences.

In contributing to the development of a transnational feminist practice, my goal is to gain some understanding of how the representation of "otherness" in literature by women can provide an opportunity for self-reflexivity, and to explore how reading across difference can promote self-growth. My purpose is not to offer a particular reading of the primary texts as the correct one, but instead to examine what these texts suggest about female self-construction of identity, the shifting alliances of identity politics, and the ability to strategically deploy subjectivities as an act of empathy and solidarity.

NOTE

[1]The term "transnational feminism" is borrowed from the anthology *Scattered Hegemonies: Postmodernity and Transnational Feminist Practices,* edited by Inderpal Grewal and Caren Kaplan. I prefer the term to "global feminism," which tends to mask difference on the basis of "nation" (in its varied constructions) and to overemphasize similarities on the basis of gender, a tendency which has historically limited Western feminism.

Acknowledgments

I wish to thank my family for their support and understanding throughout the writing of this book, even when it was not obvious that I was making any progress. My mother's nurturing and my son's enthusiasm have meant more than I can adequately express.

I am also grateful to my mentors at the Ohio State University: Debra Moddelmog for her close reading, insistence on clarity, push for excellence, challenging questions, and unfailing guidance; and Barbara Rigney, Valerie Lee, and Lupenga Mphande for their advice, patient reading, and kind support at the various stages in the development of this project.

I am indebted to my fellow students and the excellent instructors and professors in the undergraduate and graduate programs in the Department of Women's Studies for setting me on the path of feminist scholarship. Special thanks to Lori Reed for many hours of consultation and commiseration on the phone.

I also wish to thank Hampton University and the Museum for African Art (New York City) for permission to use the photograph of Ernie Wolfe III's memorial effigies.

I am especially indebted to Ikechukwu Okafor-Newsum; I would never have completed this project without his help. His absolute, unflagging belief in my capabilities was, and continues to be, a solid foundation without which I would be lost.

Illustrations

CHAPTER 1

Toward a Transnational Feminist Writing and Reading Practice

The transatlantic slave trade and the projects of exploration and development, or invasion and colonization (depending upon where one is located), have led to a contemporary global configuration in which displacement, exile, and alien domination are forces with which to be reckoned in any form of identity politics. Given such a global construction, one's geography of origin and political stance within the colonial project are inherent to the construction of identity. It is in considering the problems of identity politics and location that the binary of colonizer/colonized becomes more complicated. The issues of identity and location are problematic in the consideration of who speaks for the colonized subject. For example, questions such as the choice between the colonial language and indigenous languages as the medium for creative expression complicate any postcolonial literary practice. Balancing the collective memory of colonial victimization with a history of resistance to it becomes crucial in the attempt to create and enact, through literature, Third World solidarity across national boundaries. Furthermore, gender relations and social class complicate identity within and across colonizer-colonized populations, while at the same time providing a basis for constructing cross-cultural commonalities.

In order to reflect such complexity, the language of colonial discourse theory should be contextualized. Ella Shohat, in her clear and concise explication in "Notes on the 'Post-Colonial,' " points out that in the effort to agree upon common terminology, critics sometimes sacrifice both temporal and geographic specificity. "Postcolonial" is the most problematic of these terms, as the prefix "post" infers "after" the colonial.

1

But in many previously colonized countries, even though these have achieved political independence, economic and social colonization remain an issue. "Neocolonial" can better describe this dynamic as it indicates "colonial" but with a difference. However, the meaning of both "postcolonial" and "neocolonial" is dependent on the centrality of the colonial experience to the exclusion of all other experiences, and for that reason some critics prefer "postindependence." This term privileges the emergence of the nation-state and an achieved history of resistance. Yet "postindependence" does not seem an appropriate way to view the African American community nor other subjects of internal colonialism such as Native Americans. The first has been displaced, enslaved, and freed yet has neither emerged as an independent state nor been afforded full participation in the state which enslaved it. The second was colonized and nearly exterminated by a breakaway settler population attempting to establish its own "postcolonial" nation. Despite their own resistance efforts, Native Americans have, as yet, been unsuccessful in attempts to create a fully independent nation-state or states.

Moreover, as Anne McClintock notes, "Different forms of colonization have . . . given rise to different forms of de-colonization" (88). "Deep settler colonization" has proven to be particularly tenacious in cases such as Zimbabwe and Vietnam. The term "breakaway settler colonies" applied to the United States, Canada, Australia, New Zealand, and South Africa, elides the independence of the settlers from their center with the continuing struggle of the original populations of those lands. Further, foregrounding the colonizer-colonized binary tends to obfuscate other power relations such as the situation of women in imperial "centers" and the global economic power of the United States.

Therefore, anyone writing on matters of colonization must be careful to define his or her terms. When the word "postcolonial" appears in this book, the intended meaning is that which Ashcroft, Griffiths, and Tiffin assume in their sweeping overview of the field of postcolonial literature, *The Empire Writes Back* (1989). That is, the "post" in postcolonial should be taken to mean after the moment of initial colonization. This intentionally blurs the distinction between the colonial and postindependence periods yet leaves us with the problem of the centrality of the colonizer-colonized binary to the exclusion of other identity markers. The centrality of this binary is the very problem which is the heart of the present study and which will be consistently complicated throughout the following pages.

"Third World," as used in this analysis, refers not to a condition of underdevelopment, but rather to those countries (such as India, Tanzania,

Ghana, and Yugoslavia) who took part in or claim solidarity with the Non-Aligned Movement. The liberation movements of many of these nations viewed the Third World as a break from the capitalist and communist blocs—a third way—and achieved independence in the mid- to late twentieth century. There are, of course, problems with the move to divide global politics into three worlds. The First and Third Worlds are not monolithic: they possess historical/political differences; posing one against the other ignores issues of race/ethnicity, economic class, and gender/sexuality which affect power relations within both worlds. The Second World (the communist bloc) is currently in a state of flux and no longer wields quite the same global power. Furthermore, as Aijaz Ahmad points out in his response to Fredric Jameson's attempt to construct a "theory of cognitive aesthetics of third-world literature," the move for a First World person such as myself to use the term "Third World" can be an essentializing and politically precarious one (Ahmad 95). Nevertheless, the very idea that nonpresumptive, cross-cultural academic work is even possible is based upon being able to acknowledge and articulate difference and requires some common terminology. Therefore, I will attempt to use appropriate terms, thoughtfully chosen, for the historical, cultural situations in question.

DECOLONIZING EMPIRE: APPROACHES TO POSTCOLONIAL STUDIES

In *Culture and Imperialism* (1993), Edward Said insists that cultural production (his focus is the novel) and the hegemony of Western empire exist in a reciprocal relationship. What Said misses, however, is that in colonialist literature, empire is critiqued and reinforced in homosocial relationships between men (Prospero-Caliban, Crusoe-Friday) and in the journey into the "heart of darkness" (Conrad's Marlow, Swift's Gulliver). These masculinist paradigms often fail to engage the experiences of women trapped in the colonial project. Postcolonial literatures, often written by the subjects and former subjects of colonization, highlight the struggle against the colonial power and the impact of this struggle on the daily lives of the indigenous peoples. In approaching the field of postcolonial studies, literary critics must better attend to the ways in which colonial and postcolonial literatures address the collusion of colonialism and patriarchy, and this is one charge of my study.

Several approaches to postcolonial studies will be useful in the broader discussion of this work. One such approach is the examination of the development of "national" literatures which highlight a sense of difference on the basis of nation or region. Chinua Achebe's *Things Fall Apart* and *No Longer at Ease,* focusing on the ways Ibo traditions changed in response to contact with the West, are classic examples.

A second approach constructs similarities across national or regional boundaries on the basis of race, as black literature in the United States emphasizes the commonalities within the African world, for example, in works such as Alice Walker's *The Color Purple* (1982), *The Temple of My Familiar* (1989), and *Possessing the Secret of Joy* (1992). Such a focus in African American literature emerges in part from the Harlem Renaissance. Leaders like Alain Locke and W. E. B. Du Bois responded to nineteenth- and early-twentieth-century back-to-Africa movements and the Pan-Africanist perspective of Paule Cuffe, Martin Delaney, Marcus Garvey, and others. These transnational racial aesthetics were further strengthened by the Francophone African literary movement negritude, ascribed to Aimé Césaire and Leopold Senghor, and by the work of psychiatrist Frantz Fanon. In *The Wretched of the Earth* (1963), Fanon moves the "native writer" through the stages of proving that he or she has assimilated the colonial culture by demonstrating competence in current literary trends; to the realization that he or she has become alienated from his or her own people, triggering a period of immersion in precolonial tradition; to a "fighting phase" which results in the creation of a national, revolutionary literature. Yet Fanon is clear that despite the interdependent nature of the relations between a national culture and the creation of a nation-state—each is necessary to the survival of the other—ultimately the cultural response to colonialism must move beyond the indispensable stage of nationalist consciousness to an international, in his case Pan-African, consciousness. What the literatures generated by a Pan-Africanist consciousness have in common is their focus on the effects (cultural denigration, enslavement, displacement, identity fragmentation) of the colonial epoch upon the indigenous population and its representative diaspora.

Analyses concerned with constructing national allegories in Third World literatures, such as Fredric Jameson's "Third-World Literature in the Era of Multinational Capitalism," have galvanized our interests in the facility of colonial languages in the expression of Third World cultures. Ahmad takes issue with Jameson's move to construct a countercanon of Third World literature, a move dependent on only the literature that is available in European languages. This emphasis disregards a large body of work written and published in indigenous languages and at the same time finds in all Third World literature an explicit expression of national political interest. Jameson's proposal denies the thematic multiplicity of literature produced in the Third World and reinscribes the dominance of European languages as the foundation upon which a "countercanon" can be built. Ahmad does not fail to recognize the regional and ethnic limitations of indigenous literatures. His concern is with the tendency of the petit bourgeois literati toward canonization which inevitably favors Third World texts in colonial languages, ignoring the richness and nuances of indigenous literatures in Third World mother tongues, which contain the vast multiplicity of human experiences in the former colonies.

A third approach to postcolonial studies attempts to develop indigenous/postcolonial theories of literature which look to concepts such as "hybridity" and (linguistic) "syncreticity" as a way to reconceptualize cultural identity and to subvert Eurocentric theoretical assumptions such as "universality." Homi Bhabha's "cultural hybridity" is quite valuable to my analysis because he allows for a notion of an ongoing resistance to the hegemony of colonial power in constructing a sense of self, and provides a way to complicate the diasporic identity of a writer such as Alice Walker, who consciously creates in her fiction a link to the African homeland at the same time that she maintains a prominent "American" identity.

It is the colonized's "mimicry" of the colonizer which produces Lord Thomas Macaulay's "class" of linguistic and cultural "interpreters" between the governors and the governed.[1] But in Bhabha's construction, this colonial mimicry is more than a "narcissistic identification" with the colonizer: "[m]imicry conceals no presence or identity behind its mask" (*The Location of Culture* 88). Colonial mimicry not only produces "appropriate objects of a colonialist chain of command," but at the same time creates an "excess" which threatens colonial authority; the colonial student should be like, but not too like, the teacher. "The *menace* of mimicry is its *double* vision which in disclosing the ambivalence of colonial discourse also disrupts its authority" (88). It is out of this excess that hybridity forms. Bhabha wants to be clear that hybridity is not a "third term that resolves the tension between two cultures," not a move toward cultural relativism (*The Location of Culture* 113). Hybridity is a product of both mimicry and originary identity. The preservation of colonial authority requires an essentialist conception of the identity of the colonized to maintain the us/them construct. However, hybridity reveals the ambivalence of the symbols of English identity, which are appropriated by the colonized population, and of the English concept of an essential self, hence unsettling the "mimetic or narcissistic demands of colonial power" and reimplicating its "identifications in strategies of subversion that turn the gaze of the discriminated back upon the eye of power" (112). Distribution of the Bible translated into Hindi among the local people of Delhi in 1817 serves as Bhabha's example. The "miraculous" appearance of the "word of God" sent through an "angel" in the marketplace disguises its origins in Christian missionary ideology and obscures the attendant power relations. Yet this Christian religion becomes something else for the Indian Hindus. While the intent may have been to convert the "natives," Christianity becomes hybridized; the people accept the book as the direct word of God, denying that the English "sahibs" could have anything to say to them because the sahibs are "flesh eaters." On the basis of the Hindu dietary restriction to vegetarianism, they agree to participate in the ritual of baptism but refuse the Sacrament. The ideological tool of religion has slipped somehow. The English do not control the word: in fact, the English are read as cannibals.

However, while Bhabha imbues hybrid identity with disruptive power, he leaves the colonizer/colonized dichotomy pretty much intact. In his introduction to *The Location of Culture*, Bhabha notes that "the demography of the new internationalism is the history of postcolonial migration, the narratives of cultural and political diaspora, the major social displacements of peasant and aboriginal communities, the poetics of exile, the grim prose of political and economic refugees" (5). Yet his articulation of hybridity seems to focus on the power relations within colonialist settings. The use value of the term is in describing a strategy of resistant identity formation. But hybridity as a strategy should not be romanticized as an anti-essentialist move toward global community or applied indiscriminately across displaced populations. Bhabha is right not to sever the term from the power relations that give it birth. At the same time, "hybridity" should not be allowed to mask the relative differences among inhabitants of a diaspora. The violent cultural (and physical) disruption caused by the capture, removal, and enslavement of African people is a case in point. Ella Shohat claims that "the retrieval and reinscription of a fragmented past becomes a crucial contemporary site for forging a resistant collective identity" (109). W. E. B. Du Bois's term "double consciousness" retains the "twoness" of African American identity, yet it may collapse other identity markers, such as gender onto race. Hence, while the power relations of the colonial paradigm endure, we must also consider the particularity of each situation. So Alice Walker's criticism of African patriarchal practices is read in Chapter 4 as an attempt to retrieve a lost cultural past while creating a link with contemporary African women that is based on shared gender and race. But the impact of Walker's commentary on traditional African patriarchy has much to do with the tendency toward canonization and the global circulation of English language. Academic fascination with literary luminaries (such as Walker) who write in a colonial language subordinates, in the global flow of culture, indigenous critiques of patriarchy such as those found in the bride songs of Tumbuka-Ngoni women in southern Africa, or those mounted by various African women's groups organized to fight cultural practices affecting the health of women and children. Hence, my attention to Walker's novels is not meant to supplant the voice of African women but to cast Walker as one more voice in the chorus.

This issue of language is the battleground for many critics and writers interested in decolonizing literature. The import of the English language and its imposition upon colonized communities has given rise to a proliferation of "Englishes," both standard and nonstandard dialects. The English of Caliban is not the English of Prospero, but rather a bastard, hybrid form: the words taught to him by Miranda, combined with the "gabble" of Sycorax. Nigerian writer Chinua Achebe and Kenyan author Ngũgĩ wa Thiong'o are among the many writers and critics who outline the debate over the political and social implications of the choice of language for the production of literature and the articulation of national culture. Achebe maintains that Nigeria itself (as a country) is a creation of British colonialism; before that "hundreds of autonomous communities ranging in size from the vast Fulani Empire . . . in the north to tiny village entities in the east" populated the area. "Let us give the devil his due: colonialism in Africa disrupted many things, but it did create big political units where there were small, scattered ones before" ("The African Writer" 430). The cultural dynamics of the colonial process can, in large part, be explained by considering how the imposition of European languages indoctrinated the colonized community with ideas about labor organization, government, and social well-being under a condition of empire. In the specific case of some African states, such as Achebe's Nigeria, the English language became the lingua franca of the national bourgeoisie representative of the various national ethnicities, on the one hand, and the forces of colonialism and transnational capital, on the other. At the same time, Achebe reminds us, the imposition of the colonial language gave the various ethnic groups

a language with which to talk to one another. If it failed to give them a
song, it at least gave them a tongue, for sighing. There are not many
countries in Africa today where you could abolish the language of the
erstwhile colonial powers and still retain the facility for mutual communication. Therefore those African writers who have chosen to write
in English or French are not unpatriotic smart alecks with an eye on the
main chance—outside their own countries. They are by-products of the
same process that made the new nation-states of Africa. (430)

In the specific case of colonial languages and Third World writers,
the utility of French, English, Arabic, and Portuguese has served in the
creation of national coalitions where each national construction may
consist of many ethnic groups with distinct languages. Colonial languages have also been useful in the creation of Pan-African identity
(Africa and its diaspora) and in the global circulation of anti-imperialist
and anticolonial ideas. National languages in Africa and the Third World
exist within a complex of linguistic hegemonies which extend from the
nation-state to the global economy. Colonial languages, for the time
being, make possible the link between the economies of Third World
states and the metropoles of transnational capital. This link makes possible also the encounter of literary traditions in colonial languages. Literature is an art form and a global commodity; hence, the production of
Third World literatures in colonial languages has "colorized" colonial
languages with African, Asian, and Latin images. The production of
Third World literatures has punctured colonial hegemony while at the
same time surrendered itself to appropriation by the global market.

Ngũgĩ wa Thiongo's treatise on the question of language and literature, "The Language of African Literature," published in London for an
academic audience, does not escape the commercial monopoly of colonial languages. However, unlike Achebe, Ngũgĩ insists upon maintaining
a link between indigenous languages and literary production. Language,
as the bearer of culture, is crucial to the development of the child's self-
esteem. With the imposition of the colonial language in the educational
system, the language of school becomes divorced from the oral language
of the child's upbringing, the language of storytelling, of daily activities,
and the child is forced to embrace the language of the colonizer at the expense of a rich oral tradition. Ngũgĩ imagines a day when the national literatures of Africa are expressed in indigenous mother tongues, but does
not explain away the limitations of indigenous African languages vis-à-
vis the global marketplace. Ngũgĩ concludes this essay with an interna-

tionalist view of literature, but does not resolve the question of what language or languages the exchange of literary expression will take place in internationally. The importance of Ngũgĩ's treatise lies in his anticolonial direction; that is, the undoing of colonial relations also includes the undoing of language policies and cultural expressions that perpetuate the hegemony of colonial languages:

> I would like to see Kenyan peoples' mother-tongues (our national languages!) carry a literature reflecting not only the rhythms of a child's spoken expression, but also his struggle with nature and his social nature. With that harmony between himself, his language and his environment as his starting point, he can learn other languages and even enjoy the positive humanistic, democratic and revolutionary elements in other people's literatures and cultures, without any complexes about his own language, his own self, his environment. (28–29)

Without an educational apparatus capable of cultivating national languages in such a way that all levels of the class system are accessible, the dangerous possibility of national languages becoming a tool of the petite bourgeoisie is inevitable. H. E. Newsum illustrates this tendency in *Class, Language, and Education.* In Indonesia, Bahasa Indonesia, the former pidgin, has been appropriated by that society's elite class; the same has occurred in Malaysia, where Malay, the former pidgin, is now the national language. An aggressive peasant- and worker-based educational program is the midwife of a successful language policy. In any society, the uneven access to socially desired language skills is the result of the influence and control of the educational apparatus by an elite class. Therefore, it is only through the political efficacy of the peasant and working classes and their chosen representatives (intellectuals and educators) that such democratic access to the desired language skills is possible. Ngũgĩ suggests that

> writers in African languages should reconnect themselves to the revolutionary traditions of an organised peasantry and working class in Africa in their struggle to defeat imperialism and create a higher system of democracy and socialism in alliance with all the other peoples of the world. Unity in that struggle would ensure unity in our multilingual diversity. It would also reveal the real links that bind the people of Africa to the peoples of Asia, South America, Europe, Australia and New Zealand, Canada and the USA. (29–30)

The discussion of language choice in the production of literature is further complicated in the case of South Africa. The imposition of Afrikaans, a colonial language, at all levels of the state has been a major focus of the anti-apartheid struggle. The international and domestic cultural capital of English, also an imposed language, provides an alternative and has been strategically embraced as a tool of a unified liberation movement. Zoë Wicomb's *You Can't Get Lost in Cape Town* (1987) rehearses, in the life of the protagonist, the personal import of this political stance. Published in England and the United States, Wicomb's English-language novel of expatriation and return to apartheid South Africa, can be read as a resistance strategy played out on the international literary stage.

Ngũgĩ's emphasis on the orature of African childhood as the bearer of originary culture is echoed by the Nigerian *bolekaja* critics (Chinweizu et al.), who see African literature as autonomous from other literatures and call for writers to look to the oral tradition for a model. While what they offer to the language debate does not complicate the terrain in the same way the Afrikaans versus English issue skews the question of language, their perspective is crucial to reading African American literature. For the *bolekaja* critics, the source of literary power exists not merely in a language but rather in its reference point. The referent for all African literatures, therefore, is the African oral tradition of storytelling. Likewise, African American scholar Henry Louis Gates traces the origins of African American literature to the African folktales which survived the cultural and physical assault of enslavement. He constructs a "signifying" chain which traces the "Talking Book" from the African oral tradition through slave narratives, to Zora Neale Hurston's *Their Eyes Were Watching God,* to Walker's revision of both in *The Color Purple*. Following Gates's framework, chapter 4 develops a historical and literary context grounded in the African oral tradition for Walker's use of multiple voices in the three works in question—a completion of the circle, if you will, as evidence of her desire to speak to and for other African women.

Another approach of some postcolonial critics is to look to Marxist literary theory and apply it to Third World situations, calling for a progressive, class-based analysis which does not rely solely on race/ethnicity/ nationality but also reveals how colonialism/neocolonialism facilitates capitalist hegemony in the Third World (Gugelberger, Onoge, Newsum, Jeyifo, Ngũgĩ). In principle, the Marxist interpretation of the colonial epoch is for the sole purpose of advocating a change.[2] Hence, an analysis of multinational capitalism and the colonial superstructure complicit in its tendency toward global exploitation leads inevitably to the question of decolonization and the undoing of capitalist relations. When Aijaz Ahmad claims that socialism is the emancipatory desire of Third World people, he is echoing the Marxist understanding that at the heart of the mass's demands is communal equality as a fundamental condition for social development in the postindependence phase:

> We learn much . . . about Lamming and Achebe, Garcia Marquez and Rushdie, as their work negotiates a terrain marked by colonialism, but those same works are never examined from the perspective of socialism as the emancipatory desire of our epoch. The very terms of this discourse repress such alternative starting points, and those terms sit comfortably with the institutions—the university, the literary conference, the professional journal—which are in the business of authorizing such discourses. One would have thought that in any conflict between advanced capitalism and backward capitalism, the latter is bound to lose; socialism, therefore, has to be the third term of the dialectic, without which the antagonism of the other two terms simply cannot be resolved. If, however, socialist political and cultural practices are simply externalized out of our struggles and if those practices are located only in some ideal place designated as the second world, then a narrow nationalism can be the only insignia under which cultural production within the third world can take place or be conceptualized. (92–93)

The production and appreciation of literature have not escaped the economic hegemony of the capitalist epoch. On a consistent basis, Marxist colonial and postcolonial analyses emphasize the connection between cultural (literary) and economic production, with a view toward the decolonization of both. It is the practice of Marxist feminists to identify the interconnections between customs and their cultural expression, on the one hand, and the economy which dictates relations between the sexes, on the other. Luce Irigaray, Gayatri Spivak, and Chandra Mohanty, among other Marxist feminists, problematize the cultural and economic relations of gender and the historical complicity of traditional patriarchy as a precolonial and precapitalist form of exploitation. My concern with feminism in the following chapters is mindful of its nationalistic tendencies (bourgeois feminism, separatist feminism, and the like), seeing transnational feminism as its alternative.

My project embraces the question of national identity to the extent that such identity expresses the subjective disposition of individuals and groups. Yet a celebration of national allegory that ignores the internal diversity and discussions about language within national groups, such as Jameson does, goes against the heterogeneity of the human experience appreciated by a transnational perspective. A literary theory should address the ways colonialism and global capitalism force the intersection of experience, even against the tendency of alienation, making possible the kind of cross-cultural solidarity between colonial "centers" and their "empires" expressed in selected works of Virginia Woolf or the Pan-African paradigm orchestrated in the later novels of Alice Walker. Further, this study acknowledges the contribution of colonial languages to the potential of cross-cultural exchange at the same time as it recognizes the ground-level importance of indigenous mother tongues in the expression of a people's experience.

The forces of colonialism and capitalism have proliferated global society to such a degree that the condition of postcoloniality (postcolonial consciousness) is manifestly syncretic, representing the movement and encounters of individuals, groups, and cultures, and their participation in the global economy. Homi Bhabha's formulation of hybridity as a form of resistance takes into account the heterogeneity of individual experiences, recognizing the embodiment of multiple identities in a single subject. Hence, it is the tactical deployment of specific subjectivities based upon their strategic relevance to a specific site of struggle to which Gayatri Spivak and Chela Sandoval call attention in their discussions of Third World feminism.[3] I maintain that an understanding of and an appreciation for multiple subjectivities and the tactical deployment of specific subjectivities are necessary in the formation of a transnational feminist praxis. Therefore, each of the approaches to the field of colonial discourse theory described above will contribute to the development of a theory about the production and consumption of literature which must deal with the by-products of capitalism, colonialism, imperialism, and patriarchy in the construction of female subjectivity. Transnational feminism represents another approach to postcolonial studies, one which is capable of synthesizing the approaches referred to earlier in this section.

The idea of transnational feminism, as articulated by Inderpal Grewal and Caren Kaplan in the first chapter of *Scattered Hegemonies,* focuses first and foremost on the situation of women: "gender is crucially linked to the primary terms and concepts that structure and inform the economic and cultural theories of postmodernity" (17). The "transnational" emphasis is what allows us to move beyond narrow, localized feminisms or Third World feminisms that depend upon a center-periphery model claiming subversive potential for "marginal" positions, and beyond world-system theories that depend upon "inadequate and inaccurate binary divisions" (13). "Transnational linkages influence every level of social existence. Thus the effects of configurations of practices at those levels are varied and historically specific" (13). Therefore, a resistant feminist practice must be capable of responding to cultural oppression across all levels of social existence with historical particularity. But in addition, culture flows in many directions:

> The theories of cultural homogenization that often accompany analyses of cultural flows cannot acknowledge these historicized effects and transformations at various levels. Arjun Appadurai takes into consideration movements of people, technologies, capital, and cultures in order to describe these forces as a "model of disjunctive flow" from which "something like a decent global analysis might flow." Appadurai also warns against cultural homogenization theories, particularly those that simply equate homogenization with Americanization. His concern is that these same theories are used by nation-states to mask the fact that the threat of global commoditization is "more real than the threat of their own hegemonic strategies." (13)

Transnational feminism, therefore, allows us to view the experience of women more broadly than is possible in localized situations, while at the same time it allows us to recognize the limitations of a global perspective that tends to homogenize experience, masking historical specificity. The specific historical experiences of individual subjects and groups are indeed influenced by the international flow of capital expressed in the forms of cultural displacement, expatriation, migration, and appropriation, and transnational feminist analyses are (or should be) at all times cognizant of these realities as they manifest in identity formations.

The "democratization" of education, along with the technological advances in print media that facilitated the rise in literacy in the colonial metropoles and their colonies, make possible this transnational exchange of cultural realities in the period of late capital. Literature affords one opportunity for such exchanges. But it is not merely the exchange of culture via literary expression (the international marketing of texts) that is my concern; rather, my focus is the particular way the exchange of cultures is represented in literature and how such representations suggest common experience, empathy, and solidarity among women across cultures.

DECOLONIZING LITERATURE: CANONS
AND COUNTERCANONS

Said's concern for the production of culture and its complicity with the maintenance of empire, referred to earlier in this chapter, suggests that it is crucial to the project of postcolonial studies to identify a discourse of imperialism in the canonical literature produced at the "Centre." One tendency of postcolonial criticism pertinent to this discussion is the interrogation of colonial literature with a view toward identifying a dialectic representative of colonial domination and the potential for resistance against it, and in doing so, puncturing the colonial allegory. Such is my approach to Virginia Woolf's *The Voyage Out,* but the "seminal"[4] text of this undertaking is Shakespeare's *The Tempest* which circulates as a central metaphor in colonial discourse theory. Caliban studies, the international body of critical work on *The Tempest,* focus upon the relationship between Prospero and Caliban, especially the former's colonization of the latter through the appropriation of land ("This island's mine, by Sycorax my mother"); the erasure of the indigenous language and culture (Caliban is the "nature" upon whom "nurture" will not stick); and the imposition of colonial language ("You taught me language; and my profit on't / Is, I know how to curse . . .").

The area of Caliban studies provides rich possibilities for articulating a reading practice which can complicate the colonizer/colonized paradigm and open spaces for the construction of female selfhood. In her 1993 essay published in *Current Writing: Text and Reception in Southern Africa,* Barbara Bowen examines contemporary anticolonial productions of *The Tempest* in South Africa. She makes the point that "*The Tempest* has become a *ground* on which Third World writers meet, not because of Shakespeare's 'universality' but because writers before them have made Shakespeare's play a site for thinking about colonialism through literature" (94).

Caliban studies have taken three forms. The first attempts to locate explicit comment on the British colonial enterprise (pro and con) in the author's intent by examining the history of discourse on colonialism during Shakespeare's own period. This approach, included for example in the 1954 *Arden Shakespeare* (ed. Frank Kermode), often refers to William Strachey's reported shipwreck off "the Bermoodas" of one of the ships bound for Jamestown (officially settled in 1619) as a part of the "Virginia Project." Accounts of this wreck in 1609 may have provided inspiration for the setting and the critique of the colonial project in Shakespeare's 1611 performance of *The Tempest.*

One critic who takes such an approach is Meredith Anne Skura, who in her 1989 article "Discourse and the Individual: The Case of Colonialism in *The Tempest,*" places the writing of *The Tempest* in the colonial discourses of the time, discourses which focused mainly on the economic and romantic ends of the Europeans but which, in typical Eurocentric fashion, ostensibly ignored the existence of all people encountered in the territories these Europeans were quickly trying to claim. Strachey's report of the accidental discovery of Bermuda, for example, contained no reference to the presence of indigenous people. Skura claims that Shakespeare, in writing *The Tempest,* read Strachey's account as well as Peter Martyr's *Decades of the Newe World* (1555)[5] which describes the Spanish practice of hunting New World natives with dogs, and Strachey's account of the early Virginia colony, which devoted only one sentence to the "Indians' treachery." Skura states that, in reconstructing the colonial discourse of Shakespeare's time, "revisionist" readings of *The Tempest* which characterize it simply as "one more colonialist representation of the Other" ignore how remarkable it is that a character such as Caliban could even exist in the literary production of 1611 (57). She points out that "Shakespeare was the first to show one of *us* mistreating a native, the first to represent a native from the inside, the first to allow a native to complain onstage, and the first to make that New World encounter problematic enough to generate the current attention to the play" (58).

A second approach in Caliban studies constructs a historical overview of theatrical productions of *The Tempest,* noting the increasing emphasis on a colonial subtext, often in response to the current social climate. In a 1983 essay, Trevor R. Griffiths traces theatrical interpretations over a century, beginning with mid-nineteenth-century restorations which cast Caliban as "the poor, abject, and degraded slave . . . [a] wild and untutored creature" whose attempted rape of Miranda is understood as the revenge of a "rude and uncultivated savage [who] arouses our sympathies in behalf of those, whose destiny, it has never been, to enjoy the advantages of civilisation" (P. MacDonnell 1840, qtd. in Griffiths 160–61). This interpretation, Griffiths notes, came on the heels of the 1838 abolition of slavery in the British Empire, and it appropriated antislavery slogans. Similarly, in the 1860s the popularity of social Darwinism produced readings of Caliban as the "missing link" in evolutionary theory. A turn-of-the-century production, which depicted Caliban as "the ignorant native to whom the colonist Prospero had brought an enlightenment which he . . . spurned before learning its true value" (Griffiths 170), elicited from one critic a comparison with the "case of the aboriginal against aggressive civilisation" in Rhodesia (W. T. Stead 1904, qtd. in Griffiths 170). In response, the trade publication *Era* (October 22, 1904) satirically suggested that Caliban could just as easily be seen as representative of the "Boer nation," his intent to "people the island with Calibans" a "*clairvoyant* allusion to the [threatened] extinction of the British from South Africa by the sheer force of multiplication of the Dutch [in the early twentieth century]" (qtd. in Griffiths 172). These responses reflect the divergent thinking of the time in England concerning the predicament of aboriginal people caught in the colonial project. *Era's* satiric response conflates the victimization of Dutch settlements and that of indigenous people under British colonial authority. The attitudes that inform this thinking are similar to those which conflated the situation of Native Americans and the breakaway English settler community (under King George) during the colonial history of the United States, suggesting that the latter has more right to the land than the former.

During the European retreat from the empire in the 1950s and 1960s, few productions of *The Tempest* lent themselves to a reading of colonialism. The publication of several sociological studies utilizing the Prospero-Caliban relationship as a paradigm of imperialism (especially O. Mannoni's *Prospero and Caliban: The Psychology of Colonization,* 1950) and ongoing African independence movements, led to a 1970 revival that used black actors to play Caliban and Ariel. Caliban appears as a "detribalized field hand, with faint memories of matrilineal gods," and Ariel as the "accomplished servant who learnt European ways . . . at the end, dressing in European breeches but carrying a Kenyatta flywhisk" (Griffiths 177). A study such as Griffiths's reveals that *The Tempest* can function as a "barometer of the changing fortunes and particular relevances and resonances, critical, social, political, and theatrical of [the] themes . . ." of "colonialism, imperialism, evolution, and democracy" (Griffiths 180).

Most pertinent to my project are the approaches to *The Tempest* which point to the incorporation of the Caliban-Prospero relationship in contemporary anticolonial literatures. For example, black critical responses to Manonni's characterization of the colonized as dependent on the colonizer came from Martinicans Frantz Fanon (*Peau noire, masques blancs* 1952) and Aimé Césaire (*Discours sur le colonialisme* 1955). Césaire attacks Mannoni's reliance on the "dependency complex," noting that his psychology is far from disinterested but vested in furthering the colonial project. Fanon notes that something beyond the "unconscious neurotic tendencies" of Mannoni's "Prospero complex" lead the colonizer to both his paternalistic attitude toward the colonized and his projected fear of the rape of his daughter (Miranda) by the indigenous/hybrid man (Caliban). For Fanon, the colonial project is an economic one, a chance for "Prospero" to "grow rich quickly" (*Black Skin, White Masks* 107, 108).

Among anticolonial readings, George Lamming's *The Pleasures of Exile* (1960) bridges the critical and literary responses to Shakespeare's play. In his introduction to this collection of essays and memoirs, Lamming announces his intention to "make use of *The Tempest* as a way of presenting a certain state of feeling which is the heritage of the exiled and colonial writer from the British Caribbean" (9). Prospero's return voyage, suggested by Shakespeare in his epilogue, becomes the "tempest" beginning a new play. Lamming imagines the voyage to Milan as a dangerous one: a storm accompanies them, the crew turns mutinous, and Ariel, who has joined Prospero and company as a "privileged servant," acts as Greek chorus, commenting on the moral character of the mutinous crew. In Lamming's version, however, the focus shifts from Prospero as exiled practitioner of "Art" to Caliban, the enslaved African, whose presence on the island evokes the "triangular course of that tremendous Voyage which swept Caliban from his soil and introduced him to Heaven through the long wet hell of the Middle Passage" (12). For Lamming, the sea voyage is not the adventure of a conquistador in search of treasure nor the exile of a colonial from one "dukedom" to another: it becomes a watery "purgatory" that "lasted six thousand miles" (98). Caliban is a slave, but bearing the "seed of revolt" and carrying with him the history/future of enslaved Africans in the "New" world (98). Lamming's rearrangement of the dialogue in the play and redirection of its focus suggest a strategy of "re-presentation" that he and other creative writers explore further in later literary works.

Chantal Zabus constructs a literary history of such reworkings of the Caliban-Prospero relationship in her essay "A Calibanic Tempest in Anglophone and Francophone New World Writing." She notes that in *Une Tempête* (1969), a full-scale adaptation of *The Tempest*, Aimé Césaire imagines Shakespeare's characters in a postindependence situation, after the "tempest" of Caliban's slave revolt. Ariel becomes the "good native," whose collusion with the colonial forces makes him vulnerable to neocolonial ones. Caliban is a nationalist, who rejects Prospero's language and slave name, choosing the "X" notation of stolen identity and ending "his discourse on freedom with the powerful interjection 'Uhuru,' which

means 'independence' in Swahili" (Zabus 41). Césaire's play ends with
Prospero degenerating into madness and Caliban claiming his freedom.
Césaire imposes upon the drama contemporaneous elements of that time
when the U.S. black liberation movement and African independence
struggles prioritized the agendas of diasporic and continental Africans.
In *Une Tempête,* Césaire's appropriation of the "X" to Caliban signifies
an element of contemporary African American political practice. The
"X," which is substituted for the surname of those who are descendants
of slaves, is commonly practiced by members of the Nation of Islam, the
best-known example being Malcolm X. From Swahili-speaking East
Africa, Césaire appropriates the slogan of the independence movement,
"Uhuru." Furthermore, Zabus notes that "the resilience of the African
Caliban" resurfaces in Ngũgĩ wa Thiong'o's *Homecoming* (1972) and is
suggested by Césaire, Lamming, and C. L. R. James, who compare Cal-
iban to Toussaint l'Ouverture (the leader of a 1791 slave revolt in Haiti).
Such works utilize *The Tempest* as a place to undermine the colonial dis-
course in literature and to create important literary connections between
Africans on the continent and those in the diaspora.

While the reimagined Caliban serves African and African American
anticolonial struggles, Zabus also points out that Pierre Seguin (*Caliban*
1977) exemplifies the tendency of French Canadian writers to create a
Québécois Caliban who has been abandoned by France and colonized by
the imposition of British culture and language. She compares the Québécois and West Indian adaptations in their concern with "the predicament
of the writing Caliban whose subject is the liberated Caliban but whose
medium is Prospero's language" (49). Zabus concludes that, at its best,
"adaptation and re-interpretation of the earlier Old World literature
of colonization, i.e., *The Tempest,* as literature of decolonization is . . .
superior in effectiveness to an anti-colonial polemic . . . [and] constitutes
one of the most cogent strategies of decolonization in literature" (49).

While the central position that the *Tempest* metaphor marks in my
own analysis reveals a reliance on it as a strategy of decolonization of literature produced at the Centre, it is to be seen as only one possible strategy. Anticolonial, "polemic" literature produced by formerly colonized
peoples and those whose work stands in solidarity with them constitutes
another strategy of decolonizing the field of literature studies. Additionally, the failure to question the absence of the indigenous peoples from
contemporary re-visionings of the play reflects the tendency, referred to
earlier, to equate colonial tyranny against a settler class (Canadian
French and South African Dutch) with that of the silenced indigenous

people. In *The Tempest* and re-presentations of it, the tension between presence and erasure revolves around the indigenous community. This absence is addressed, however, in Lamming's chapter "In the Beginning" in *The Pleasures of Exile*. He laments the disappearance of the indigenous Carib and Arawak Indians from "Caliban's" island. A "blind, wild forest of blood" was born out of the "fantastic human migration" of "criminals," "defeated soldiers," and "Royalist gentlemen," following the economic promise of that "mischievous gift, the sugar cane," a gift that required the importation of enslaved Africans to turn a profit. So while *The Tempest* functions as an essential metaphor that echoes through the field of postcolonial studies, providing a rich language for an anticolonial reading of canonical literary work, Lamming's "hybrid" text reminds us that the economics of the colonial project, that is, the appropriation of bodies and material resources for profit, has been at the core of the urge to colonize and should never be far from our analysis of the cultural production of Western empire. However, the collusion of Miranda and her literary sisters in the cultural production of imperialism and their potential in an anticolonial, antipatriarchal discourse are given little attention in colonial and postcolonial analyses.

WHEN IT RAINS IT POURS: WOMEN OF *THE TEMPEST*

As *The Tempest* has provided a site of struggle for the aforementioned postcolonial writers concerned with decolonizing canonical literature and constructing transnational solidarities, Shakespeare also functions as a point of connection for some contemporary African American writers; John Edgar Wideman's novel *Philadelphia Fire* (1991) is one example. His reworking of *The Tempest* attempts to open a space in the play for the female character Miranda to speak. (It should be understood that the choice of texts upon which this chapter focuses is, in part, arbitrary. Yet it is not the primary texts in and of themselves that constitute a theory about literature. It is the issues they raise, the questions they ask, the spaces they open that make them useful tools of a transnational feminist critical practice.)

Wideman's re-presentation of *The Tempest* is inundated with the colloquial vernacular of contemporary black Philadelphia and is foregrounded by the May 13, 1985, attack by the Philadelphia police upon the Move Organization's headquarters at 6221 Osage Avenue.[6] Wideman's "tempest" is not one of water but of fire, which he uses as a metaphor for the bombing. Wideman's *The Tempest,* the play inside the

novel, is rehearsed but its public debut never takes place. His main character, Cudjoe, remembers a summer in 1968, when having decided to
produce a rewriting of the drama, he gathered his students with the idea
of teaching them *The Tempest* from a critical perspective as preparation
for beginning rehearsals. It is through Cudjoe's teaching of the play that
Wideman articulates a black perspective and the gender politics of this
would-be colonial discourse.

Cudjoe's teaching of *The Tempest,* from the outset, indicts the Eng-
lish language in the colonial project: "The lingo is English landwich.
Quack of the baddest, biggest Quacker. King's English. Pure as his tribe.
We've heard it before, leaking from a circle of covered wagons, a laager
squatting on the veld, a slave fort impacted on the edge of a continent . . .
Queen's English to be more exact" (Wideman 129). In his indictment,
Wideman's protagonist suggests the evolution of bastard, hybrid tongues
which are the product of empire making and the language of Caliban,
who is the godfather, according to Cudjoe, of his intended audience and
students. In Cudjoe's version of the play, Caliban's language is not only
an altered derivation of the King's English (imparted to the indigenous
character through the colonial daughter), but a de-Anglicized and decol-
onized stream of meanings which allow a counterhegemonic voice to
flourish in a colonial discourse:

> Him broken my island all to pieces. . . . Walls dem all fall down fall. . . .
> All fall down on golden sand of this island mine.
>   Or was mine. Once pon time. . . . Mine by way Queen Sycorax
> my mother. Him say all dat and say my mother am witch. Why him
> play dozens now? Say my mother dead in nother country. . . .
>   Noting make self. I be her son and son of some fader. Don't try
> guess who. Don't say in de play. I no know, no want to know. Just want
> island back. Queen Mama back. No time be playing dozens now. (121)

On the matter of women, Cudjoe's teaching of *The Tempest* opens up
a discussion of female roles in the play. Through Cudjoe, Wideman calls
attention to the silencing of women's voices, first by calling attention to
the sketchy references to Sycorax in Shakespeare's original version and
again by privileging anticolonial critics of the tendency of the Prospero-
Caliban metaphor to underestimate Miranda's complicity in the occupation of the island by outsiders. For example, in one scene, Cudjoe resists
the idea offered by a white friend, Charley, who wants to rewrite Prospero's character as a liberal who repents his bad deeds and returns owner-

ship of the island to Caliban. Cudjoe refuses to hear Charley's suggestion because, once again, the homosocial relationship between the would-be liberal colonial patriarch and the subjugated "other" leaves out any significant role for the play's female characters. With vested interest, Charley opposes Cudjoe's desire to bring Miranda "forward, to the edge of the stage . . . framed by the proscenium arch . . . [to] transform this moment of the play to a soliloquy by bringing her stage front, by directing Prospero her father and Caliban her suitor manqué to drift subtly away and back, a fog dissipating as she slides forward" (130).

Timbo, Cudjoe's old college friend, also denounces the idea of providing Miranda with the opportunity to speak. He believes that Miranda is so co-opted by her father (her words are his words) that there is no hope for her character as a liberatory force against the colonial project of the play. The role that Cudjoe suggests for Miranda is an ambiguous one. On the one hand, he acknowledges to his students the "dangerousness of this speech about speech shoved in a woman's mouth" (140). Once Miranda is brought forward and the men are banished to the far ends of the stage, "the men subside; they are less than they thought, less than we thought, than she thought, less at the center of this speech than some editors have thought who ignored Miranda's claim, attributed the words about to be spoken to her father" (139). On the other hand, Cudjoe recognizes the female voice as untenable in the literary tradition of a patriarchal society. While it is his wish to give Miranda some semblance of self-determination, the historical inevitability of her complicity in her father's doings reveals that Cudjoe's wishes are romantically ambitious:

> She's trying her best to be her own person. She wants to share. But she can't. She's a prisoner, too. Hostage of what her father has taught her. A language which Xeroxes image after image of her father, his goodness, his rightness, his deed to the island and the sea-lanes and blue sky and even more than that. The future. Which is also confirmed and claimed in the words he taught her and she taught Caliban, buried of course, unmentionable of course, like her private parts, but nonetheless signified in the small-print forever-after clause of the deed. Her father needs her to corner the future, her loins the highway, the bridge, sweet chariot to carry his claim home. Her womb perpetuates his property. (141)

In this verbal tug-of-war between the three male characters, Cudjoe, Timbo, and Charley, Wideman satirizes the issue of silencing female voices in canonical literature and in the subversive responses to it.

Wideman goes further by calling attention to the economics of gender politics and the role of the colonial daughter in the exchange of property. But Wideman's concern about the place of women in his re-presentation of *The Tempest* does not turn solely on the colonial daughter. As Wideman's Caliban reveals in the speech quoted above, in Shakespeare's play it is only through Prospero that we learn of Caliban's mother:

> . . . This damn'd witch Sycorax,
> For mischiefs manifold, and sorceries terrible
> To enter human hearing, from Argier
> Thou know'st was banish'd; for one thing she did
> They would not take her life. . . . (1.2.264–267)

Sycorax is not present in the play to tell her own story; why she was banished "with child" from Algiers to the island, and what it was she did that saved her from being executed, are not revealed. Nor do we know anything of Miranda's mother; again, the character with the knowledge is Prospero and he reveals as little as possible. After he asks her what she remembers from the time before they came to the island, when Miranda was three, Prospero proceeds to explain their situation to Miranda but in indirect language:

> PROSPERO. Thy father was the Duke of Milan and
>   A prince of power.
> MIRANDA. Sir, are not you my father?
> PROSPERO. Thy mother was a piece of virtue, and
>   She said thou wast my daughter; and thy father
>   Was Duke of Milan, and his only heir
>   And princess no worse issued. (1.2.53–57)

While his explanation of the "foul play" which left him and his daughter banished and his brother Antonio in power in Milan is quite direct, Miranda's absent mother, like Caliban's dead one, marks silenced female voices in Prospero's narrative. Nor does Wideman embellish the play by filling these gaps. He does, however, expose the absences while imagining an explanation for Caliban's desire to people "this isle with Calibans" (1.2.351). Wideman's Caliban says to Miranda:

> I know plenty curses already. See because while you pouring all that
> nice poison in my ear, your daddy shipping my island piece by piece

back to where it won't do me a bit of good. You neither, quiet as it's kept. Never met your mama. Nothing against her. For all I know she might be my mama, too. So I ain't playing the dozens but that lying ass wanna be patriarch Prospero who claims to be your daddy and wants to be mine, he's capable of anything. Incest, miscegenation, genocide, infanticide, suicide, all the same to him. To him it's just a matter of staying on top, holding on to what he's got. Power. A power jones eating away the pig knuckle he was dealt for a heart. All this fancy talk don't change a thang. Cut him loose while you still can. (142)

Wideman's Caliban puts no stock in Prospero's explanations of his own or Miranda's parentage. His main concern is the loss of his land, and he knows Prospero is capable of the vilest of acts to displace him from what he feels is rightfully his by birth.

Through Cudjoe, Wideman engages in a familiar political and theoretical practice in the study of women in literature which is an important part of my own theoretical framework, that is, the search for female selfhood. The "political correctness" of this practice is complicated by facts of objective history and ideology (the colonial economy and patriarchy). What is problematic here is that we cannot escape the conditions into which we are born. We are not governed merely by our social conscience, but also by the social/material conditions that govern all relationships. A reading practice that perpetuates an ideology and does not recognize, at the same time, the social/material conditions of characters and writers is a naive one. A responsible reading of literary texts recognizes not only the players of the narrative, and the adverse forces that surround them and their victimization, but also their complicity in this state of affairs and therefore the measure of their liberatory potential. In order for Cudjoe's Miranda to speak, he must successfully produce Caliban's dramatic defeat of Prospero's colonial project. In order for Caliban to defeat Prospero, Miranda must see her father for the patriarch he is and recognize the parallels between her own subjugation and that of Caliban as well as her own complicity in that subjugation. By linking Miranda's success to Caliban's, Wideman provides us with the fundamental relationship of feminism to anticolonialism. But Cudjoe's play is never produced; Cudjoe's attempted revision is set in 1968 and grows out of the black liberation struggle which tended to totalize identity under the banner of race and submerge women's issues beneath race-based demands, assuming that the best strategy focuses on one issue at a time.[7] It is only Wideman's 1990 examination of African American collective action in the late 1960s that is capable of envisioning the absolute necessity of coalition and of expressing a kind of empathy across identity markers called for by contemporary feminists.

TRANSNATIONAL FEMINISM
AND ANTICOLONIAL READING

Black feminist bell hooks, in *Yearning: Race, Gender, and Cultural Politics* (1990), suggests that our ability to empathize with the circumstances of others gives us the vehicle to bridge whatever gaps exist between women of different nationalities, classes, and sexual identities, and also between different communities of women and men regardless of their location in the global economy. Methods for creating and deploying empathy, as a first step in cross-cultural relations, have been offered by a long line of feminist scholars and/or activists. Bernice Johnson Reagon suggests that before one can participate in the hard work of coalition building, one must "take the time to construct within yourself and within your community who you would be if you were running society. . . . At a certain stage nationalism is crucial to a people if you are going to ever impact as a group in your own interest" (358). From that point, however, one must move outward if one is to survive in the larger world. Crucial to this move is "allowing people to name themselves. And dealing with them from that perspective" (367).

For filmmaker Trinh T. Minh-ha, the starting point is a stance that allows difference "not opposed to sameness, nor synonymous with separateness," to replace conflict. "[D]ifference is not what makes conflicts. It is beyond and alongside conflict" (372). In "Not You/Like You: Post-Colonial Women and the Interlocking Questions of Identity and Difference," she suggests that "difference" can be a "tool of creativity to question multiple forms of repression and dominance" (372). Trinh recommends that we move beyond essentializing, that is, thinking that there is an "insider" who can be depended upon to know and represent her community, as this position is both false and untenable; too frequently the "insider" becomes restricted to speaking only for that community for which she is "expert." A theory of subjectivity should refuse "to naturalize the I" and reveal "the myth of essential core," creating instead "a ground that belongs to no one, not even to the creator," where subjects can relate across difference, acknowledging our interdependency (374).

For Gloria Anzaldúa, this ground is the borderlands/*la frontera,* the literal border between what is now called the United States and Mexico, as well as the metaphoric border between two different, often conflicting identities. The mestiza subjectivity she claims straddles Anglo, colonial Spanish, and indigenous cultures, enacting one or the other at any given time but always conscious of the contiguous and overlapping existence of all three. *La facultad,* the capacity to sense what is below the surface and to respond accordingly, facilitates this process. This skill is latent in all of us but most developed in "those who do not feel psychologically or physically safe in the world" as a first line of defense (38).

Anzaldúa suggests that a mestiza consciousness can move beyond the two or more cultures it straddles to create "a new mythos—that is, a change in the way we perceive reality, the way we see ourselves and the ways we behave. . . . The work of *mestiza* consciousness is to break down the subject-object duality that keeps her a prisoner and to show in the flesh and through the images in her work how duality is transcended" (80). While she recognizes that a "proudly defiant . . . counterstance" is a "step toward liberation from cultural domination," it is not "a way of life." "A counterstance locks one into a duel of oppressor and oppressed. . . . All reaction is limited by, and dependent on, what it is reacting against" (78). Yet in recommending that the mestiza develop a "tolerance for ambiguity" and a "pluralistic mode" of operation in the world, Anzaldúa emphasizes the importance of self-examination—of sorting out what aspects of self are inherited, acquired, and imposed, and of returning to one's literal and figurative home (79). The cultures of one's "home" must be made a conscious part of this self-construction.

Working from within the geography of home and family, Argentinean feminist María Lugones, for example, suggests that acknowledging that those who are the closest to us exist in worlds which, although they may overlap with ours, are also discrete from ours is the first step in seeing them as whole people. In Lugones's construction, we each inhabit several overlapping "worlds" and are capable of experiencing others. Yet she draws a distinction between "agonistic" traveling into others' worlds —that is, traveling as a conqueror—and "loving" world traveling (400). Entering the world of someone we identify with is an attempt to "understand *what it is to be them and what it is to be ourselves in their eyes.* Only when we have travelled to each other's 'worlds' are we fully subjects to each other" (401).

What hooks, Johnson Reagon, Trinh, Anzaldúa, and Lugones recognize in common is that the "self" is a construction and as such our sense of self is permeable. Anzaldúa suggests that her border status facilitates an identity politics that allows her to imagine coalitions across identity categories:

> As a *mestiza* I have no country, my homeland cast me out; yet all coun-
> tries are mine because I am every woman's sister or potential lover. (As
> a lesbian I have no race, my own people disclaim me; but I am all races
> because there is the queer of me in all races.) I am cultureless because,
> as a feminist, I challenge the collective cultural/religious male-derived
> beliefs of Indo-Hispanics and Anglos; yet I am cultured because I am
> participating in the creation of yet another culture, a new story to ex-
> plain the world and our participation in it, a new value system with im-
> ages and symbols that connect us to each other and to the planet.
> (80-81)

While the theory of multiple identities that these feminists articulate allows for individual agency, at the same time it does not lose the embod-
iedness of the self. Bell hooks and Bernice Johnson Reagon emerge from
African American communities; Trinh T. Minh-ha's "difference" springs
from and moves beyond an essential Asian identity; Gloria Anzaldúa embraces Chicana lesbian existence within a mestiza body. Each recognizes
that the aspects of identity which are common to others of her community, and on which basis the community is oppressed, must sometimes
form the base of a "counterstance" or a sense of "nation."

In the "essentialism" versus "constructionism" debate, what the
raced and gendered body means in terms of access to relative power, access to resources, material, aesthetic, and otherwise, is the crucial part of
constructionism. The raced female subject is overdetermined from without. The reclaiming of female and racial selfhood by such a subject is a
defining moment calling for a self-determined conception of personhood
marking the binary between insiders—the community, the commune, the
collective, the nation—and outsiders whose perpetrations deny this self-
definition. The act of self-definition is an essentializing moment. Like
the fighting phase in Fanon's construction of national culture, gender to-
talizes identity just as, at moments, race, ethnicity, and statehood may be
totalizing identity markers.

The systems of patriarchy and colonialism promote various stages
of development which constitute individual selfhood beginning with the
stage of assimilation. To be specific, assimilation as used in this analysis,
refers to the ideological co-optation of oppressed subjects by their op-
pressors. The assimilated woman is the unselfconscious product of the

collective functioning of the hegemonic patriarchal culture. It is the as-similated subject who will support, upon her narrow shoulders, the pil-lars of patriarchal domination and imperialist exploitation. But this stage is followed by her conscious recognition of the essentializing restrictions of the body, the constructed hierarchy of social relations, and the over-lapping presence of the two. Through the encounter with difference, at this second stage of development, the subject realizes that her own iden-tity is determined by her relationship with the men of her community and in relations to those outside her community upon whom imperialist dom-ination has been administered. Such are the relations between daughter and father, between black and white of shared class, and between poverty and wealth on the issue of gender. Like the child who must determine who she is and is not through the touch and visual reflection of those around her, or the black girl who must figure out her blackness in relation to white domination and thus seeks solace in racial unity, the "assimi-lated" woman who realizes her complicity with the colonialist patriarchy must figure out her location. In doing so, she often looks for a space be-yond the cultural in a "pure or original femininity, a female essence, out-side the boundaries of the social and thereby untainted (though perhaps repressed) by a patriarchal order" (Fuss 2). The next phase beyond nar-row feminism recognizes the interrelationship between would-be nation-alistic or essentialized identities. This third stage makes possible coalition building based upon feelings of empathy across identity cate-gories, that is, differences.

The overlapping presence of difference penetrates the historical force of narrow feminism and nationalism as it reveals itself to individu-als and groups as the most fluid determinate of social interaction. Differ-ence exists not only in the spaces between subjects but also cohabits in the common spaces we occupy, and within each of us. Female selfhood and racial selfhood live as co-occupants in the house of subordination with its other progeny, the downtrodden classes, the elderly, the sexually tabooed, and the physically challenged. In this house, narrow nation-alisms may encounter the "joining." While history presents us with ex-amples of how difference begets antagonism, cohabitation in the house of subordination solicits our "profound desire for social solidarity," our profound desire to "join" (Bhabha 18). In the house of art and fiction, that is, in the folds of creative imagination where it is possible to enter-tain difference without fixed polarities, such a "joining" may take place. Our imagination is pricked by our desire to "join" in the process of read-ing texts, which on their own accord challenge us to cohabit in worlds beyond our daily experience, to see pieces of ourselves in the lives of others, to see them in our lives, and to see them and ourselves as they see us. This act of imaginative reading can open up an "interstitial passage between fixed identifications . . . the possibility of a cultural hybridity that entertains difference without an assumed or imposed hierarchy" (Bhabha 4). The potential for such a reading is provided by Alice Walker's creative imagining in *The Temple of My Familiar,* a novel which solicits us to consider the boundless possibilities of selfhood and community across the would-be fixed barriers of time, race, gender, family, nation, age, and sexual identity. Such exploration is also facilitated in Toni Morrison's "Recitatif," a short story which imagines the lives of two girls of pointedly different but unrevealed races, a strategy which, Elizabeth Abel notes, allows a reading experience where "Sameness coexists with difference, psychology with politics. Race enforces no absolute distinctions between either characters or readers, all of whom occupy diverse subject positions, some shared, some antithetical" (495). By permeating the narrative with a psychological struggle that "crosses difference"—the ambivalence of the mother-daughter relationship— "Recitatif," according to Abel, disrupts the dialectic of racial difference and "complicates, without cancelling, both its narrative of difference and the differences in reading that this narrative provokes" (495). To the extreme ends, the act of reading texts, of suspending self-contained judgment, opens us up to stories such as Morrison's *Beloved,* which considers infanticide as an act of murderous love. Rarely is such openness practiced in our real day-to-day experience, except when a writer like Morrison compels us to consider with our minds and hearts the real-life experience of someone like Margaret Garner.[8]

These texts by Walker and Morrison intervene in the engaged reader's "normal" life, and such intervention "introduces creative invention into existence," that is, it increases our ability to transform and invent ourselves appropriately as we encounter different subjective realities (Bhabha 9). This kind of invention has proven difficult in a society fractured by transnational capitalism. Any such undertaking is always met by the overarching moment of our subjectivities. The homeless, for example, are not "othered" simply because they are without shelter, but they are incarcerated in the technological epoch of constricted opportunity perpetrated by multinational capitalism.

The processes of intervention and invention, to which Homi Bhabha alludes in the introduction to *The Location of Culture,* concern also the business of what to do about the perpetrators of antagonistic history—the engaged breaking of and break with the material/ideological institutions, both public and private, of antagonistic history. A transnational feminist reading of texts like *The Temple of My Familiar,* "Recitatif," and *Beloved* demands the reader's self-examination of where we stand with those antagonistic institutions and challenges us to live our lives accordingly. It challenges us to form a liberatory praxis in which we act as well as envision a future.

INTERVENTION AND INVENTION AS TRANSNATIONAL FEMINIST PRACTICE

The anticolonial compulsion expressed in the reworkings of *The Tempest* by postcolonial writers represents one kind of writing practice that seeks to break with antagonistic history. The work of contemporary feminist literary artists like Morrison, Walker, Woolf, and Wicomb represents a next stage in the construction of a liberatory writing practice that not only genders the binaries of race and colonial oppression but also, among its best examples, complicates identity construction with a matrix of overlapping identities. This writing practice and its corollary reading practice, as means of understanding the intersections of gender and colonialism, grow out of oppositional political strategies (proletarian movements, feminisms, nationalisms, gay liberation movements, etc.) and examine the ways in which they interrelate. These transnational feminist discursive strategies are interventionist in nature, proposing a form of political action that intervenes in the narrow spaces of subjectivity constructed as oppositional, and creates interstices of possibility with a view toward bridging the gaps between narrow forms of nationalism. Such interventions are beneficial to the oppositional centers (narrow nationalisms) and the differential subjectivities within them because such interventions create the potential to stave off the continuation and reproduction of subjugation of one subjectivity by another. Chela Sandoval, in her essay published in the spring 1991 issue of *Genders,* provides a psychological profile of this kind of intervention which she calls a "differential" consciousness in opposition:

> It is in the activity of weaving "between and among" oppositional ideologies . . . where . . . oppositional consciousness can be found. I have named this activity of consciousness "differential" insofar as it enables movement "between and among" the other equal rights, revolutionary,

supremacist, and separatist modes of oppositional consciousness considered as variables, in order to disclose the distinctions among them. In this sense the differential mode of consciousness operates like the clutch of an automobile: the mechanism that permits the driver to select, engage, and disengage gears in a system for the transmission of power. . . . [D]ifferential consciousness . . . functions as the medium through which the "equal rights," "revolutionary," "supremacist," and "separatist" modes of oppositional consciousness became effectively transformed out of their hegemonic versions. Each is now ideological and *tactical* weaponry [tactical subjectivity] for confronting the shifting currents of power. (14)

Sandoval's differential consciousness, and the understanding and empathy which I am suggesting are needed in the reading of literary texts, call upon us to move beyond the aesthetic concerns of literature. But while Sandoval's focus on U.S. Third World feminism as a model recognizes the limits of U.S. bourgeois feminism, the heterogeneity of the U.S. women's movement, and the potential for coalition, it fails to recognize the relationship of U.S. Third World feminists to their "motherland" communities (the diasporic consciousness of Asian, African, and Latina women) and how these relationships constitute the international exchange of culture and politics. A theory of transnational feminism therefore must also be capable of articulating *trans*-national connections among women

Arjun Appadurai calls for each of us who are concerned with this business of constructing responsible approaches to problems of postmodernity to theorize the complexity of the current global economy, and the disjunctures between economy, culture, and politics. In "Disjuncture and Difference in the Global Cultural Economy," he asserts that an adequate theory of global cultural exchange must articulate a more complex process than is reflected by the master narratives of Western feminism, center-periphery models of colonial and neocolonial power, migration theory, or neo-Marxist global development theory (328). Appadurai's landscape metaphor outlines a topography of interrelated currents and power shifts in the global flow of capital, human subjects, technologies, culture, and ideologies made possible by the rapid communication of meanings and images available in the late twentieth century. The encounters and intersections of this traffic bring about the contestation and solidarity between and among various subjectivities.

An example of such encounters and intersections can be seen in "Little Steven" Van Zandt and Artists United Against Apartheid's "Sun

City" project in the mid 1980s. The "Sun City" project merg
human rights radicalism with the anti-apartheid movement via the circu
lation of meanings and images, "truth to educate," in the forms of a
record album (including inserts and fact sheets), a companion book, and
a music video (Mphande and Okafor-Newsum 21). This "Sun City" project exemplifies an interventionist strategy and a postmodern phenomenon which disrupts the authoritarian and hegemonic discourses of U.S.
international policy and the entertainment industry and attempts to
bridge the gap of nationalisms in the United States.

Intervention that creates ruptures and disjunctures in authoritarian
discourses (any discourse that becomes reified, whether it be hegemonic
or counterhegemonic) reinterprets traditional cultural forms and disrupts
neocolonial oppression through the strategy of invention:

> The borderline work of culture demands an encounter with 'newness'
> that is not part of the continuum of past and present. It creates a sense
> of the new as an insurgent act of cultural translation. Such art does not
> merely recall the past as social cause or aesthetic precedent; it renews
> the past, refiguring it as a contingent 'in-between' space that innovates
> and interrupts the performance of the present. The 'past-present' be-
> comes part of the necessity, not the nostalgia, of living. (Bhabha 7)

However, traditional modes of behavior and representation are useful
only in as much as they advance the contemporary differential subjectivities which exist in and between individuals and groups. The authority of
tradition must give way to the shifting relations of power and the equal
rights of all human beings. Traditions that authorize patriarchal power,
for example, must be transformed out of their tendency to reify the masculine subject.

The African American *vigango* carvings (sing. *kigango*) of Neo-
Ancestralist[9] artist Ikechukwu Okafor-Newsum are interventionist in this
very way (see Figure 1.1). In his project, Okafor-Newsum disrupts the
conventional east African discourse of the Mijikenda patriarchy, creating
in his art a nonpreferential representation of gender while stylistically
appropriating the Kenyan *vigango*. Patterned after the work of Kenyan
artists such as Ernie Wolfe III (see Figure 1.2), Okafor-Newsum's
kigango effigy of Harriet Tubman is a deliberate intervention in the masculine preference reflected in the artistic tradition of the Chama ya Gohu,
a secret male society of the Mijikenda. Like Wolfe, Okafor-Newsum has
carved these *vigango* over a period of time; unlike Wolfe, whose work

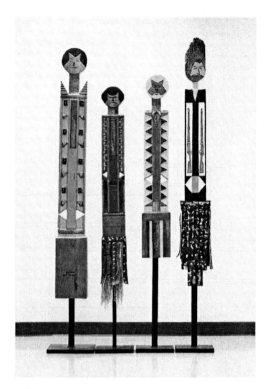

Figure 1.1. African American *vigango,* Columbus, Ohio. Wood, paint, natural pigment, fiber. H 68 in.–80 in. Ikechukwu Okafor-Newsum, Neo-Ancestralist, 1994–95. From artist's personal collection. (Photo by Robert Landrum)

represents the more traditional form, Okafor-Newsum memorializes his own female maternal ancestors. In this project, Okafor-Newsum advances the value of resistance politics and cross-gender solidarity in the celebration of both a traditional art form and, in the example pictured here, a female champion of human rights from antebellum U.S. history. Okafor-Newsum's *vigango* effigies represent also the progressive intersections of race in the human rights struggle in his rendering of the Euro-American U.S. antislavery activist John Brown. These carvings offer a "newness" while appropriately retaining traditional modes of expression, and in this way these works demonstrate how "intervention" in the

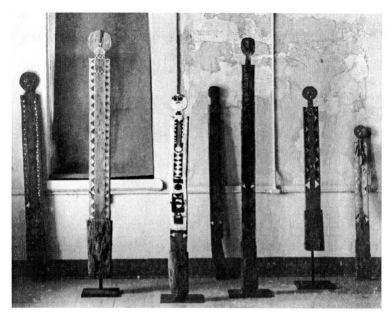

Figure 1.2. Memorial effigies, Mijikenda, Kenya. Wood, pigment, plaster, cloth. H 52 in.–80¼ in. Ernie Wolfe III, 1978–85. Hampton University Museum In New York Center for African Art, *ART/Artifact: Art in Anthropology Collections* (Munich: Prestel Verlag, 1988) 147.

form of creative imagining begets invention in the construction of collective identity.

Unlike Wideman's "failed" attempt (Cudjoe's production never takes place), the interventionist strategy of Van Zandt represents successful anticolonial action in the world of music; Okafor-Newsum's work represents a successful subversion of patriarchy in the world of visual art. Furthermore, Okafor-Newsum's *vigango* carvings, like Alice Walker's imaginings of African people in her work, invent a connection to a lost cultural history. Walker's novel *Possessing the Secret of Joy* and the related documentary film *Warrior Marks* (including her published journal chronicling the making of the film) represent another example of intervention that disrupts the authority of tradition and patriarchy, provoking both conflict and solidarity among women occupying the same racial identity but whose national and cultural identity mark their difference. Although *Possessing the Secret of*

Joy evokes controversy, I will show in chapter 4 that it also opens a space for new alliances between diasporic and continental Third World women and disrupts the narratives of Western hegemonic feminism and traditional patriarchy. Such alliances represent what Frantz Fanon claims is the appropriate project for the anticolonial cultural worker: "to use the past with the intention of opening up the future, as an invitation to action and a basis for hope" (*Wretched* 187).

In imagining a reading practice that can accommodate an identity politics which addresses the eruptions of feminism, race politics, and class struggle into the late-twentieth-century narratives of global capitalism and the legacy of colonial domination, we must consider the contexts that merge in the process of literary interpretation. Between the writer and the reader stands the text, which carries with it all of its "reproductions" in the Benjaminian sense: "The uniqueness of a work of art is inseparable from its being imbedded in the fabric of tradition. This tradition itself is thoroughly alive and extremely changeable" (Benjamin 225). A most striking example is the text referred to earlier in this chapter, *The Tempest*. Whether read or performed, the "readings" of this play are dependent on the interplay between the text and the context of its reproductions. Current reworkings of the play, such as in Wideman's novel, often depend on the reader's awareness of more traditional adaptations of the play for their very meaning.

The focus on an exploration of the context of the author-writing act is not to attempt to reconstruct authorial intent. It should, instead, reveal what the relationship between the author and his or her work says to us, the readers. For example, how do Virginia Woolf's critical essays, in which she claims that, as a woman, she has no country, influence how we read her satiric portrayal of the British colonial mind-set in her fiction? How does knowing that Zoë Wicomb identifies herself as a black South African, rather than deploy the "Coloured" title assigned under apartheid, inform how we read her exploration of the privilege her "Coloured" protagonist exploits by expatriating to England? And what does knowing that Alice Walker re-creates a psychic connection to the African continent as an intervention into the disruption of the slave trade say about her construction of African people in her novels? It is the goal of my project to entertain these questions.

Also a factor in any "reading" of literature is the context of the reading subject. Complicating the reading act is the acknowledgment that, as reader of literature trained in academic feminism, I may be predisposed to an oppositional stance. The criticism that Gayatri Spivak makes in

"The Problem of Cultural Self-Representation" of a popular form of reader-response theory is that it assumes a community of readers without questioning the political investment or relative power of that community: "the political element comes out in the transaction between the reader and the texts. What I am most insistent upon is that the politics . . . of the reader should be put on the table as scrupulously as possible. Textual criticism cannot just be a judgement on the basis of disinterested readings by a presumed community " (50). An awareness of one's own location provides a base from which to "travel" to the "world" of another. A sense of "otherness" is unavoidable when reading outside of one's own experience, but as suggested earlier, this sense of difference need not be accompanied by unexamined value judgments. This project rests on the premise that the authors whose novels serve as primary texts for the next three chapters have something to contribute, across differences in epoch, geographical origin, race, and other differences in individual life experience, to the development of a transnational feminist reading practice.

My aim is to demonstrate, through critical application, a transnational feminist reading of texts. In participating in such a practice, we must be critically cognizant of our own location in master narratives and in reified subjectivities. Our embrace of postmodernism must be more than an aesthetic understanding; rather, we must see the postmodern in terms of global power shifts. We must recognize the tendency of nationalism to subsume multiple subjectivities with a view toward working ourselves through and out of such narrow boundaries and developing the ability to tactically deploy our various subjectivities appropriately. The goal of the imagination should be invention, and as such our senses must be sharpened and our actions vigilantly directed at the myths that determine our social relations: tradition and fundamentalism must be stripped of their deterministic powers. The state of our postmodernity and our postcoloniality is continually changing and expanding, encompassing our very being. It is not that we have moved to a place somewhere beyond modernity or colonialism, but rather that these histories remain with us in our present, and inevitably they influence, one way or another, the direction of our future.

NOTES

[1]See Macaulay's "Minute on Indian Education," written when Macaulay was Legal Member of Council to the General Committee on Public Instruction in India, 1835. It was his recommendation that the focus of the colonial education

system in India should be to teach English, to "make the natives of this country good English scholars" because "English is better worth knowing than Sanscrit or Arabic"; neither of these languages has any "peculiar claim to our encourage-ment" as either "languages of law" or of religion. The law and religion of which he is speaking refer, of course, to those imposed by Britain.

[2]In the case of literary interpretation, Marxism demands a rethinking of the moral imperative conveyed in literary texts suggesting that the critique of the capitalist epoch and the desire for socialism have also a tradition in literary ex-pression. Jack London's *Iron Hill,* Chinua Achebe's *No Longer at Ease,* Ayi Kwei Armah's *The Beautiful Ones Are Not Yet Born,* Virginia Woolf's *Three Guineas,* Ngũgĩ wa Thiong'o's *Devil on the Cross,* and Sembene Ousmane's *Xala* serve as examples.

[3]Spivak, in her introduction to *Subaltern Studies,* uses the term "strategic essentialism" in a very similar way to Sandoval's "differential consciousness in opposition," which is addressed in more detail later in this chapter.

[4]The use of the masculinist term is intentional here; it reenacts the masculin-ist focus of these early applications of the play to the colonial dynamic.

[5]This date also marks the arrival of the first slave ship in the West Indies, the *Good Ship Jesus,* a Spanish vessel.

[6]Move was a local black cultural nationalist group whose existence was deemed a threat to the gradual assimilation of (a few) African Americans into the existing city power structure. In a house besieged by bullets, water cannons, and high explosives, eleven people (six adults and five children) died. In the resulting fire, fifty-three homes in the predominately black community were destroyed, leaving 262 people homeless.

[7]This critique is most compelling in the autobiographical writings by women like Elaine Brown and Assata Shakur, who are former Black Panther Party members.

[8]Margaret and Robert Garner, their four children, and Robert's parents crossed the Kentucky-Ohio border in January 1856. Their story appeared in the *Cincinnati Daily Enquirer* in a series of articles beginning on January 29, 1856. Having sought temporary shelter at the home of a free African American, the family was overcome by the posse who had been pursuing them. By the time the pursuers gained entry into the barricaded house, one child was dead, two others injured, and the mother was holding a "heavy shovel" over the head of the fourth. Margaret Garner was indicted for the murder of her daughter. Rather than be re-turned to Kentucky under the Fugitive Slave Law of 1850, "Margaret Garner pre-ferred to remain in Cincinnati so that her children could be free, even if it meant a murder trial" (Cynthia Griffin Wolff 115).

[9]Neo-Ancestralism is an art movement conceived by African American artists Tom Phelps, Jimi Jones, and Ken Leslie and born in Cincinnati, Ohio. This trio came together with a clear agenda about the mood and method with which they wanted to approach their work; group cohesion and reference to Africa's influence on Western art are the starting point from which they create. Following the philosophy of Alain Locke which advises looking to Africa for inspiration, and the example of AfriCobra (Chicago 1968), the Neo-Ancestralists combine African cosmology with African American material culture in installations that examine the diverse dimensions of African American existence.

CHAPTER 2

Virginia Woolf: A Critique from the Center of Empire

In the past four decades, former colonies of European imperial powers have fought for and attained political independence. Yet, as Edward Said notes, "imperialism . . . lingers where it has always been, in a kind of general cultural sphere as well as in specific political, ideological, economic, and social practices" (*Culture* 9).[1] It is to this contested general cultural sphere that literary interpretation belongs. In this (not quite) postcolonial era, literary criticism which endeavors to resist arrogant world traveling must begin by acknowledging the complicity of colonial literature with the practice of empire and the ways in which our favorite literary works of that epoch either reinforce or criticize that practice.

This chapter will examine how a sample of Virginia Woolf's extensive body of work both engages in and critiques the practice of empire through her textual encounter with patriarchy. To call Woolf a "colonial" writer, of course, raises issues of periodization—her work is claimed as modernism, a "post"-colonial distinction. However, as the previous chapter makes clear, in terms of the global economy, postcoloniality is not yet accomplished: the players may have changed, but the game is much the same. In terms of the creation and consumption of literature, twentieth-century literary practice continues a colonial discourse begun earlier.

Modernist works such as E. M. Forster's *A Passage to India* (1924) engage themes of earlier colonial literature such as Rudyard Kipling's *Kim* (1901): Kipling's romanticized Indian landscape becomes threatening in *Passage;* both novels are concerned with the practice of surveillance as part of everyday life in the colonies and with a subtext of mutiny; and both racialize Indian identity—Kim can "transcend" this construction because he is really "white," whereas Aziz (*Passage*) cannot. But while Kipling seems more interested in the development of a good colonial administrator, Forster begins to question the presence of the colonials in India; India becomes, in Said's term, a "stage" onto which Europe's concerns about itself are displaced. Later Indian writers writing in English often respond to *Passage* by focusing on the indigenous people of India, pushing against the homogenizing effects of colonial writers. For instance, Mulk Raj Anand, born in India and educated there and at Cambridge, creates a protagonist from the lowest caste in *Untouchable* (1935), stepping beyond an Indian-English racial construction to a recognition of caste/class and religious differences, as well as the effects of modernization on Indian people.

As indicated in chapter 1, my own choice of primary texts for this project is somewhat arbitrary; other writers might prove to be fertile ground for an analysis of colonial discourse generated in the Centre. But to the end of articulating the beginnings of a transnational feminist writing practice, Virginia Woolf seems a particularly apt choice. She is, in many ways, at the center of the Centre. At the time during which she was writing, Woolf circulated among the leftist intellectual elite of England. Both of Virginia (Stephen) Woolf's parents had family ties to the colonial service in India. Leonard Woolf resigned his commission in Ceylon, both because he was beginning to doubt the justice of the British colonial enterprise and so that he could remain in England when Virginia agreed to marry him. Virginia Woolf, with her brother, Thoby Stephen, a Cambridge-educated attorney, began a Thursday night discussion group which evolved into the esteemed Bloomsbury intellectual and artistic community. Hogarth Press grew from this community as an outlet for publishing work which they considered progressive. Although the publication of her own novels spans only slightly more than twenty years of a life cut short by mental illness and suicide, Virginia Woolf was celebrated during her lifetime as a successful author.

Her success, the prominence of her intellectual circle, and the influence of the contemporary women's movement on the academy, have led to her work being adopted fairly quickly into most constructions of the Western literary canon. As Western feminism has concerned itself with urging the academic industry to take women's literature seriously, a transnational feminist practice that concerns itself with the discourse of colonialism must demand attention to the critical stance of canonized work at the same time that it calls attention to the large body of non-

Western literature. Woolf's short stories are consistently anthologized by publishers such as Norton. A glance at *Dissertations Abstracts International* indicates hundreds of dissertations in which Virginia Woolf is listed as a subject, beginning in 1950, nine years after her death. Harold Bloom's "elegy" to *The Western Canon* (1994) lists five of Woolf's novels (*Mrs. Dalloway, To the Lighthouse, Orlando: A Biography, The Waves,* and *Between the Acts*), and devotes an entire chapter to an analysis of *Orlando*.

And not only has her literature gained some stature in traditional canon constructions, her extended essay, *A Room of One's Own,* has been a foundation of the contemporary (Western) feminist movement. The demand for a "room of one's own" as a metaphor for the time and space needed for women's creativity echoed through 1970s consciousness-raising groups in the United States. The essay continues to appear on syllabi for many women's studies classes, and Woolf's work constitutes a significant area of academic study for feminist scholars in women's studies and English departments, spawning courses, conferences, and publications. But whether the "canon" in question is that of Western civilization or of academic feminism, "Canon building is Empire building" (Toni Morrison, "Unspeakable" 8). Thus, Virginia Woolf occupies an insider-outsider position vis-à-vis the academy: her work appears both within the traditional canon and in feminist studies, a field whose claim to "outsider" status is founded on an ideology of oppositional consciousness, an ideology which Woolf embraces by claiming outsider status in her book-length feminist tract *Three Guineas* (1938). The notion of canon building as empire building, and the participation of women's literature in this enterprise, is a contradiction within oppositional politics that cannot be easily avoided. It is with this understanding that a transnational feminist reading practice must critically and actively negotiate the nationalistic tendencies in feminist discourses.

Because of Woolf's position at the center of Western academic feminism, it is crucial to examine her contribution to a late-twentieth-century discussion of colonial discourse in women's literature. Woolf's critique of women's social, economic, and political position in patriarchy is her point of entry into this discussion. Denied access to the formal higher education of her brothers, Woolf was ever conscious of this lack. Still, she managed to educate herself with her father's help, using his extensive library and taking occasional courses in Greek and Latin, privileges afforded her by her family's upper-middle-class status and her access to leisure time. Such social status in a capitalist economy always rests upon the exploitation of others' labor. Whether she was cognizant of her complicity in such exploitation in her real life and how committed she was to the kind of socialism espoused by her husband remain matters of debate and are not my concern in this project. However, it is the position of this chapter that *The Voyage Out* and *Between the Acts,* the two novels that frame Woolf's career, recognize this complicity. Begun in 1907 and published first in 1915 as *Melymbrosia, The Voyage Out* (1920) reflects an epoch during which England's hegemony had not yet been challenged. Its nascent critique of the connections between patriarchy and international tyranny are further sutured in reading Woolf's later work. Her book-length essay *Three Guineas* and her final novel, *Between the Acts* (1941), emerge from a period when fascism was on the rise in Europe, and England was in the way. While resisting the attempt to reconstruct authorial intent, this study will examine how readily available biographical information, along with Woolf's popular nonfiction work *A Room of One's Own* and *Three Guineas,* informs our contemporary (re)readings of these novels and reveals Woolf's awareness of her complicity in the imperialism of which she is critical. Woolf opens a discussion that later writers have continued, placing gender fragmentation in a larger social context.

The Voyage Out is Virginia Woolf's first novel. Her provocative use of silence as a theme of the narrative is one of the keys to recognizing Woolf's self-critique in the novel. Silence in *The Voyage Out* is not the voicelessness that Eve Lynch attributes to working women in *Mrs. Dalloway* and *To the Lighthouse* (Lynch 68–75). Nor is it the "unsaid" which Patricia Laurence explains as "something one might [feel] but does not say" (Laurence 1) and which Woolf often demonstrates as interior dialogue, especially in her central female characters. This silence in *The Voyage Out* represents a critical stance. Toni Morrison reminds us that "invisible things are not necessarily 'not-there'; that a void may be empty, but is not a vacuum. In addition, certain absences are so stressed, so ornate, so planned, they call attention to themselves; arrest us with intentionality and purpose, like neighborhoods that are defined by the population held away from them" ("Unspeakable" 11). The purposeful use of silence in *Voyage* points not to an inability to speak but to a refusal to speak for colonized populations. The contribution of this refusal to a transnational feminist literary practice must be examined.

While there are many ways of reading *The Voyage Out,* most of the critical work to this point seems to focus on the voyage as a metaphor for an individual journey. Within such a perspective, the main setting of the novel—South America—is simply background, or more interestingly, an "alien culture" against which the white British protagonist, Rachel Vinrace, attempts to define her feminine role, in part through her relationship with Terence, a fellow visitor from England. Reading the Third World setting as providing the opportunity to construct First World subjectivity opens up the question of whether we can justifiably read this novel without a critique of Britain's colonial project, a project in which Woolf's own family took part. The question must be asked, Does Woolf replicate the project which Said criticizes in his earlier anticolonialist work *Orientalism;* that is, does she use the racialized and colonized "other" to construct the identity of the dominant, colonial "self"?

As far as this chapter is concerned, *The Voyage Out* partakes of the same kind of individual self-indulgence and "othering" as seen in other texts of its type. However, the practice of using the "other" to construct the identity of the self is not performed in Woolf's novel without a self-reflexive critique of empire. This chapter holds that the silencing of indigenous voices and the relative absence of the indigenous presence in the narrative of *The Voyage Out* make a rendering of the colonial critique more difficult and indirect as compared to the more popular approach of seeing the text as a female bildungsroman. But attempting to uncover in the text a critique of the colonial project is a viable interpretive undertaking, an interpretive strategy demanded in the late twentieth century of those who are critical of the global construction of former colonization and continuing imperialism, and facilitated by a transnational feminist approach to literature. Such a critique leads to one very important contested site—the issue of speaking for others—to which this chapter will speak. Woolf's tendency toward silence in *The Voyage Out* invokes a kind of reading of the narrative which raises the question of who can speak for, or "about," the other. Linda Alcoff, in her essay "The Problem of Speaking for Others," forces this distinction by demanding that in speaking "for" others we must recognize that "the discursive context is a political arena," and speaking for others is a political act in which we must first interrogate our locations as speakers (15). Woolf's deliberate refusal to articulate indigenous voices in her novel suggests, despite her complicity in colonial literary tradition, the possibility of a keen awareness of that position, a transnational feminist awareness "that one's privileges in the world-system are always linked to another woman's oppression or exploitation" (Grewal and Kaplan 19).

"[T]HE THINGS PEOPLE DON'T SAY": SILENCE AS A CRITIQUE OF EMPIRE IN *THE VOYAGE OUT*

An interpretation that recognizes the possibility of Woolf's self-reflexive critique of the colonial project is absent in many of the earlier feminist critical appraisals of *The Voyage Out*. Critics often privilege the bildungsroman as a master narrative for Woolf's novel, and Joseph Conrad's *Heart of Darkness* as a model of this master narrative, over a postcolonial reading of *Voyage*. However, the tendency of postmodernist critics to read *The Voyage Out* as a feminist subversion of patriarchal master narratives while ignoring the indigenous backdrop of empire reinscribes uncritically the colonial project. In such analyses, European feminism assumes the character of master narrative.

For example, according to Gilliam Beer, *The Voyage Out* represents an early effort by Woolf to explore the impact of eternal "nature" on women. Nature is the sign of Darwinian evolution with the South American jungle as Rachel's laboratory of self-metamorphosis.[2] This master narrative approach, which fails to take account of the boundaries of cultural nationalism, is further inscribed by John Bayley's approach to the text as a critique of gender roles among the British elite, a critique which does not imagine the significance of Woolf's interrogation of Western female privilege in the Third World context.[3] Like Bayley's, Pamela Transue's feminist critique of *The Voyage Out* is marked by a provincial interpretation of women's roles in heterosexual relationships among the British elite, oblivious to the protagonist's location vis-à-vis the indigenous community surrounding their resort.[4] Transue's reading of *The Voyage Out* situates feminist development on the body of the British heroine, Rachel, and privileges the roles of women in European society with a lack of awareness for their present geographic location in the text: the South American jungle. But the fact that the characters of the novel very consciously locate themselves psychologically and physically outside and above the indigenous environment should signal attention to the narrative subtext, suggesting to the reader the relationship of colonial subjects and colonized objects. The little England that is constructed in the hotel parlor is a colonial outpost in a "heart of darkness." What is lacking in these critics' interpretations of Woolf's *The Voyage Out,* that is, the acknowledgment of the complicity of this female bildungsroman in the colonialism of England, also perpetrates a master narrative approach.

The heart of darkness, as represented in Howard Harper's chapter on the novel, suggests to us the dismal existence of women in heterosexual marriage.[5] But it is also a metaphor in a signifying chain whose immediate referent is the journey in Joseph Conrad's *Heart of Darkness,* a search for an unknowable, indescribable primeval self, often read by indigenous colonial discourses as a master narrative of Western imperialism. These approaches conceal the colonizer-colonized paradigm and reveal the tendency of feminist criticism toward nationalism, presuming that only the women of the First World struggle to overcome patriarchy. Such a tendency denies the potential for self-interrogation and participation of First World women in a process leading toward the decolonization of Third World women and their societies. Hence, a critique of the colonial project in Woolf's *The Voyage Out* requires some understanding of the way in which silencing the narrative, social and ideological voices of indigenous subjects calls attention to the alienation and objectification of the colonized, and how Woolf's thematic performance of this silencing, along with the protagonist's death at the end of the novel, might serve as a site from which we can view Woolf's critique of the colonial project.

Silencing in Woolf's *The Voyage Out* is not a diminution of indigenous being but rather a strategy of resistance against the appropriation of difference. Woolf resists speaking for the other; her project is not one of paternalistic caretaking. A close reading of *The Voyage Out,* instead, reveals her appreciation for the everyday reality of the indigenous women, and she does so without imposing Western feminist ideology upon them. One might then read a kind of transnational feminist approach in Woolf's embrace of the indigenous female characters in the novel. Such a reading echoes bell hooks's "radical postmodernist" position "which calls attention to those shared sensibilities which cross the boundaries of class, gender, race, etc., that could be fertile ground for the construction of empathy—ties that would promote recognition of common commitments, and serve as a base for solidarity and coalition" (*Yearning* 27).

Scenes in *The Voyage Out* that frame the everyday lives of indigenous women call to the reader's attention a strategic deployment of gender awareness that crosses cultural boundaries, even as they demonstrate Rachel's distance from these women. Rachel Vinrace's encounter with the indigenous female represents Rachel as being among, as Appadurai states, "persons who constitute the shifting world in which we live: tourists, immigrants, refugees, exiles, guest workers, and other moving groups and persons [who] constitute an essential feature of the world and appear to affect the politics of (and between) nations" (329). It is important to see Rachel Vinrace and her accompanying entourage as "ethnoscapes" whose movement from center to empire involves the import of cultural baggage, the replication of their imagined community (the mother country), and for whom the act of travel is a cathartic exercise preoccupied with individual rites of passage. Through these characters, Woolf impregnates the narrative with ideas of heterosexual romance and marriage, and with empty spaces, "the things people don't say," that represent gaps in the master narrative of patriarchy and empire. The act of travel in *The Voyage Out* mimics Marlow's journey from the mother country to empire, and his trip upriver into the "heart of darkness." But Woolf breaks with the colonial master narrative invoked by Conrad by creating a kind of self-reflexivity in Rachel. Indeed, the surface similarities of the two texts are so striking that they can support a reading of *Voyage* as a transnational feminist response to *Heart*.

In the first place, the opening scene of *The Voyage Out* resembles that of Conrad's *Heart of Darkness*. Both share the setting of London and the Thames. *Voyage* shows us Helen and Ridley Ambrose as they stroll along the river in anticipation of their voyage out of daily life in London to enjoy a sabbatical in South America; Marlow, Conrad's narrator, sits with his friends on the *Nellie* at the "sea-reach of the Thames" waiting for the "turn of the tide" (Conrad 17). In spite of the similarities, the ways in which Conrad and Woolf alert the reader to the particular class identity of the main players in their narratives is a clue to their different approaches to constructing the colonial subject. We know something of Marlow's class identity via a straightforward description of his friends and peers with whom he sits—The Lawyer, The Accountant, The Director. Conrad's class markers are conveyed through direct signification; however, the language that identifies the class position of the Ambroses is much more subtle.

It is, instead through indirect signification that we come to understand how Helen and Ridley Ambrose, in this first scene, walk together separated by social class from the others present. They walk arm in arm although the sidewalks are very narrow, causing "lawyers' clerks [to] have to make flying leaps into the mud; young lady typists [to] have to fidget behind [them]" (Woolf 9). Mr. Ambrose's height and Mrs. Ambrose's blue cloak set the couple apart from the "small, agitated figures . . . decorated with fountain pens, and burdened with despatch-boxes, [with] appointments to keep" and a "weekly salary" to draw (Woolf 9). The Ambroses' class status is not directly associated with professional titles, such as lawyer, accountant, or director; rather their physical stature, appearance, and way of moving about in their world establish their class position. The way in which the two authors represent the social divide of the class system is also key in understanding how the main characters in the respective texts are representative of colonial agents once they arrive at the tropical settings of Africa and South America.

In both instances the European travelers enter into the indigenous societies as representatives of the hegemonic colonial power. And whereas Conrad attempts through direct signification to construct the identities of his characters out of their unique difference from the indigenous population, Woolf, through indirect signification, constructs the identities of her characters by demonstrating the indigenous absence, evoking the subtext of "otherness" which remains buried below the surface of her narrative. So critics often see Rachel on a voyage to her "heart of darkness," that is, toward her fate as a female victim of patriarchy. But Rachel avoids this abyss when she dies of an unnamed illness with which she has become afflicted while on the upriver excursion reminiscent of Marlow's trip up the Congo. Rachel's death also cuts short other possibilities suggested in Woolf's subtext. The possibilities I will examine here connote "otherness," but not only the gendered otherness which crosses cultures: these possibilities include otherness internal to European patriarchal societies. While my reading will attempt to demonstrate the dialectic between the female subject of patriarchy and the "primitive" subject of the Third World "other," it will be my goal also to expose the possibilities/life choices that function as centrifugal forces within Western patriarchy.

In *The Voyage Out,* Woolf provides at least four examples of female existence in white Western patriarchal society. Through the characters of Helen, Miss Allan, Evelyn, and Rachel, we are presented with four uniquely different models. While Rachel is a young woman who must be ushered into English society and hence into mature womanhood, the others serve as different models of female life choices. In short, and in stereotypical terms, they represent the loyal and devoted wife, the spinster, and the unmarried and financially independent flirt. Helen is described as strong and independent, yet she caters to her husband; she pursues her social life with the crowd at the hotel, while she sees that his survival needs are met so that Ridley can continue to write. From the opening paragraphs of the novel, her possibilities within the marriage are circumscribed: when Helen will not allow Ridley to comfort her, he stalks off; she breaks away, daydreams while staring into the river, yet "she knew she must go back to all that" (Woolf 11). Although she has misgivings about the impending journey, she must carry on with the proper role of wife.

The models Woolf offers for single female lives are no more appealing. In opposition to Helen is the somewhat older Miss Allan. While Helen's life revolves around her husband, Miss Allan has never married. She makes her living by writing, and her goal for this vacation in South America is to complete a history of "all" literature written in "the King's English." In this community, Miss Allan's single status sets her up as an eccentric; her friendly overtures to Rachel seem slightly threatening. The other single female character is Evelyn, who wants to be friends with the men in her life and cannot make up her mind which of her suitors to marry. She seems to want more than just a marriage, and plans to form a club devoted to "social good." However, when it becomes apparent that she will not settle down with a man, Evelyn's reputation suffers. The narrative conveys to the reader the terrifying limitations imposed upon these women, and it is the fate of these women which Rachel avoids by dying. But another possible reading of this construction of female role models would recognize that the patriarchal society of which Rachel and the other female characters are victims is also a colonial society. In this reading, Rachel's South American "heart of darkness" encompasses the possibility of the political kinship of female victims of imperialist patriarchy and the indigenous victims of colonialism.

Jane Marcus suggests this kinship in her analysis of *The Waves,* Woolf's 1931 "experimental antinovel" (137). In describing the novel as the response of a "socialist, feminist, and pacifist" to both a familial and cultural history of participation in the colonial project, Marcus suggests that the subordination of women under patriarchy can be likened to the subordination of colonized populations under imperialism (137). This assessment provides clues to interpreting Woolf's first novel as an earlier exploration of this complicity, thus reading in Rachel the possibility of a certain self-reflexive potential.

Marcus tells us that it was Woolf's grandfather James Stephen who "invented the family metaphors that locked colonial subjects into the roles of infantilized bad children in relation to a benevolent 'Mother Country'" (148). She argues that Woolf's grandfather infused the philosophy of imperialism with the culturally inscribed tenets of the patriarchal family, rewarding the complicitous female members with power over servants in a replication of the master-servant relationship. Of *The Waves* Marcus asserts that

> The study of the silenced colonial other and the search for the subaltern
> voice, while not articulated in Woolf's text, do lead us to recognize the
> power of the white woman's critique of herself and her social system,
> and of the complicity of English literature with imperialism and class
> oppression, especially when such a critique is not to be found in the
> writing of modernist men. (143)

Marcus's observation of the silenced colonial other and the search for the
subaltern voice in *The Waves* suggests how silence contributes an indirect discourse on colonialism in *The Voyage Out.*

In *Voyage,* the phallocentric construction of womanhood is represented in direct signification, but the Western construction of the Orientalized other, in an indirect way, also plays prominently in the manner in
which Woolf's characters construct themselves. The Orientalized other
(Said, *Orientalism*), as an object of a discursive practice, lies at the deep
structure of Woolf's narrative and functions subliminally in the mind of
the reader who is vested in a postcolonial reading. It is important to bear
in mind who these European travelers are: they are a generation among
several generations of Europeans, privileged by upper-class status and a
romantic imagination of cultural superiority born out of a binary relationship with non-Europeans and manifested in the projects of imperialism and colonialism. The fetish of Orientalism at the time of the text's
production was woven into European societies. Despite the class and
gender hierarchy within Western society, European selfhood constructed
an imagined superiority in oppositional relations to the subordination of
the Orientalized other.

This kind of Orientalism connotes, as Said puts it, not the people or
places of the Far East, as the term is popularly used, but rather an ongoing discourse based first on the imaginative writings by the West about
the East in the form of creative literature, travelogues, missionary tracts,
anthropology, and the like. This discourse is further developed in colonial literature of the period of Europe's excursions into Africa, South
America, the Caribbean, and Australia, as well as Asia. Said's term provides postcolonial critical theory with a metaphor for the power dynamics of colonialism and patriarchy and their reinforcement in literature.
Said makes the point that these

> ideas, cultures, and histories cannot seriously be understood or studied
> without their force, or more precisely their configurations of power,
> also being studied. To believe that the Orient was created—or, as I call

it, "Orientalized"—and to believe that such things happen simply as a necessity of the imagination, is to be disingenuous. The relationship between Occident and Orient is a relationship of power, of domination of varying degrees of a complex hegemony. (Said, *Orientalism* 5)

The binary events of power and domination which describe the relationship of patriarchal and colonial power, on the one hand, and feminized and Orientalized powerlessness, on the other, describe the "horror" in the "heart of darkness" which is Rachel's bildungsroman. Such a reading of *Voyage* considers both the direct and indirect signifiers of patriarchal and imperialist domination respectively. Woolf does not put words in the minds and mouths of her characters that signify colonial domination. It is the silence in the text which echoes the binary relationship between the European traveler and the colonized other. Rachel's voyage into womanhood takes place within the macrocosm of the European colonial project in which feminist consciousness is an internal discourse and colonialism is the external discourse, silent and yet present in the reader's imagination.

In contrast, the discourse of Orientalism is a more direct practice in Conrad's *Heart of Darkness*. On only three occasions is the binary relationship of privileged white traveler and indigenous nonwhite other conveyed directly in *The Voyage Out*. But in Conrad, the Orientalized other is denied wholeness and is characterized by synecdoches of difference— for example, the "burst of yells, a whirl of black limbs, a mass of hands clapping, of feet stamping, of bodies swaying, of eyes rolling" which Marlow encounters on his voyage up the Congo (Conrad 50); "a black figure . . . on long black legs, waving long black arms . . . [with] horns" (81); and "swaying scarlet bodies with horned heads" (83) who approach as Marlow's company is leaving. *Heart of Darkness* is full of such references. The peculiar way in which race and gender work together in this novel equates the indigenous woman with the sexualized jungle. The narrator recalls a woman who seems to have had some personal connection to Kurtz and who comes to the shore as the boat is pulling away, taking the desperately ill Kurtz out of his heart of darkness:

And from right to left along the lighted shore moved a wild and gorgeous apparition of a woman.

She walked with measured steps, draped in striped and fringed cloths, treading the earth proudly, with a slight jingle and flash of barbarous ornaments. . . . bizarre things, charms, gifts of witch-men hung

about her, glittered and trembled at every step. She must have had the
value of several elephant tusks upon her. She was savage and superb,
wild-eyed and magnificent; there was something ominous and stately
in her deliberate progress. And in the hush that had fallen suddenly
upon the whole sorrowful land, the immense wilderness, the colossal
body of the fecund and mysterious life seemed to look at her, pensive,
as though it had been looking at the image of its own tenebrous and
passionate soul. (Conrad 76)

In this representation, it is difficult to tell where the body of the woman
ends and the jungle begins; moreover, her "worth" is measured in the
product these imperialists are harvesting from the jungle—ivory.

In *The Voyage Out,* however, it is only when Rachel peers out of a
window of the hotel and looks down on the "wrong side of hotel life" that
an indigenous presence is first signified directly (252). Rachel sees three
women sitting amid the trash strewn outside the hotel kitchen door,
speaking Spanish and plucking chickens for the evening meal. Their
identity is marked by gender, language, and their socioeconomic position
as menial laborers there to serve the hotel guests. The reader's attention
is drawn once again to the indigenous presence during the excursion that
Rachel, Terence, and the others take upriver to visit the "primitive"
village to observe "native" life and to purchase artifacts. In Woolf's
description of this event we see the second direct reference to the Orientalized other:

Stepping cautiously, they observed the women, who were squatting on
the ground in triangular shapes, moving their hands, either platting
straw or in kneading something in bowls . . . the women took no notice
of the strangers, except that their hands paused for a moment and their
long, narrow eyes slid round and fixed upon them with the motionless,
inexpressive gaze of those removed from each other far, far beyond the
plunge of speech. Their hands moved again, but the stare continued . . .
as they sauntered about, the stare followed them, passing over their
legs, their bodies, their heads, curiously, not without hostility, like the
crawl of a winter fly. As she drew apart her shawl and uncovered her
breast to the lips of her baby, the eyes of a woman never left their faces,
although they moved uneasily under her stare, and finally turned away,
rather than stand there looking at her any longer. . . . But soon the life
of the village took no notice of them; they had become absorbed into it
[as Kurtz had been immersed in the heart of darkness]. The women's

hands became busy again with the straw; their eyes dropped. If they moved, it was to fetch something from the hut, or to catch a straying child, or to cross the space with a jar balanced on their heads; if they spoke, it was to cry some harsh, unintelligible cry. (284–85)

While Conrad's "wild and gorgeous apparition of a woman" is the "image" of the "passionate soul" of the "immense wilderness," the "colossal body of the fecund and mysterious life" that is Marlow's Africa, Woolf's focus is the activity of the indigenous women and their response to the intrusion of Rachel's party. Their "gaze" is "motionless, inexpressive," and cannot be decoded by the Europeans. Their "stare" is "not without hostility." Marlow constructs a fantasy about the indigenous woman he observes—an intimate connection with Kurtz and with "witch-men" who have hung "barbarous ornaments" on her. Rachel, on the other hand, cannot comprehend what she sees—the women inhabit a place "far beyond the plunge of speech," where the only sound heard is "unintelligible." What is "beyond the plunge of speech" are the actual voices of the indigenous other—the utterance which Woolf refuses to put in the mouths of the hotel workers. As Rachel turns away from the sight of women plucking chickens at the hotel, on the trip upriver she and her companions turn away from the nursing mother's stare. In both of these examples, the direct reference to the indigenous other refers mainly to female subjects; in this way Woolf collapses gender identification and colonial subjugation onto the female body, and it is a construction which cannot be fully comprehended by Rachel and her female companions.

In the third instance in which the Orientalized other is directly signified, we are able to glimpse the social fragmentation of the colonized society. Here enters a male doctor who attends Rachel during the brief period of her fatal illness. Dr. Rodriguez is a local resident and is either of the Spanish settler class or a member of the native petite bourgeoisie, but in either case he does not possess the cultural capital of English language, a lack which affects his status among the visiting British colonials, none of whom speak Spanish. In this scene, Woolf reverts to indirect signification by introducing French language as a kind of lingua franca shared only by the doctor and the character Terence. Rachel is thus denied speech or narrative consciousness during the doctor's bedside visits. The scene is significant in a postcolonial reading of the text because it echoes the complicity of colonial languages in empire, while at the same time it alerts the reader to Rachel's inability to speak. As Rachel's individual fate is in the hands of two men, the fate of the colonized population is often determined by the two-headed creature of patriarchy and colonialism and articulated in an imposed language.

As these are Woolf's only direct references to the colonized other, for the most part otherness is a function of what is not said in her narrative. Woolf gives silence thematic importance in her text via the discussion Terence has with the others in this little British enclave about the novel, *Silence,* that he is writing. Rachel indicts the utility of writing literature if what one wants to do is to communicate feelings. She asks, "Why do you write novels? You ought to write music. Music . . . goes straight for things. It says all there is to say at once" (212). The narrative voice seems to agree. This community, according to the narrator, provides "excellent material . . . for some chapters in the novel to be called 'Silence, or the Things People Don't Say,' " especially at the point in the novel at which the growing involvement between Rachel and Terence becomes apparent to the reader (220). Helen suspects Rachel has a secret but does not ask; Rachel is aware of having a secret but has not yet admitted to herself that she is in love. There is a lot of frantic activity at the hotel, as it is the height of the season, but very little real communication among the guests. Silence even overcomes the couple when they first acknowledge to each other their love: "Not only did the silence weigh upon them, but they [are] both unable to frame any thoughts" (271). They begin to walk through the woods and "[t]he silence [is] again profound" (271). Terence asks Rachel if she enjoys his company; she says she does and then "[s]ilence seem[s] to have fallen upon the world" (271). They continue "to walk for some time in silence" and finally admit to each other "We are happy together . . . We love each other" (271). The deeply personal confession "I love you" is never spoken; rather their unspoken acceptance of couple status within this little England becomes the focus of this scene. The character Terence, his literary project, and the narrative attention focused on the difficulty these colonialists have in expressing their most personal feelings constitute "silence" as a theme of Woolf's novel. Woolf's thematic focus on "silence" is accompanied by unresolved ruptures in a narrative of feminine development: Rachel's voyage toward the "heart of darkness" is part and parcel of the larger project of domination and subordination.

Rachel cannot speak of this horror when she looks from the hotel window, sees the female servants outside the kitchen door, and looks away. But it is the manner in which she looks away which suggests to the reader her disillusionment and/or discontent, albeit ambiguous, with the British colonialist social system. At this point in the novel, Rachel observes indigenous women, one in particular of advanced age, slaughtering a chicken:

> The blood and the ugly wriggling fascinated Rachel, so that although she knew that someone had come up behind and was standing beside her, she did not turn round until the old woman had settled down on the bench beside the others. Then she looked up sharply, because of the ugliness of what she had seen. (252)

The narrative here suggests Rachel's fascination with "the blood and the ugly wriggling," and therefore it is difficult to discern the "ugliness" that Rachel has seen. Is the ugliness, in fact, the slaughter of a chicken or "the wrong side of hotel life"? The ambiguity here is another form of indirect signification, a double entendre. The colonial critique or the critique of social difference based on oppression is blurred but also made possible by the duality of meaning embedded in the narrative. Such a reading of this scene places the colonial critique inside the head of Rachel and not in the mouths of the indigenous other.

Hence, Woolf avoids the dangers inherent in this practice of speaking for others. The focus of the colonial critique in *The Voyage Out* is Woolf's own complicity as a British subject and daughter and granddaughter of men who were very directly involved in the colonial project. This is where Woolf's colonial narrative differs from Conrad's master model. Marlow questions the morality of the economic and physical oppression of the indigenous African population, but Conrad does not acknowledge his own complicity. While we cannot read Marlow and Conrad as one and the same, we do know that Conrad himself made a very similar voyage; the autobiographical aspects of *Heart of Darkness* are difficult to deny. Conrad's awareness of his own complicity in the colonial project is ambiguous at best. While his narrator may articulate some concern for the effects of the company's "noble cause" on the people of Africa, Conrad's unselfconscious, exoticized representation of Marlow's (and Kurtz's) "other" fails to deconstruct the imperialist tendency of colonial literature. Marlow returns successfully from his journey into the heart of darkness; Rachel is not allowed to return. Marlow delivers Kurtz's report, "The Suppression of Savage Customs," to the company, visits with Kurtz's intended, and continues his life as a seaman. The novel ends as it opens: Marlow shares his tale with his companions, including the Director of Companies, as they embark upon yet another journey accompanied by the ghosts of earlier "adventurers and . . . settlers; kings' ships and . . . dark 'interlopers' of the Eastern trade" (19).

But Rachel's encounter with the colonial project in the heart of darkness is accompanied by a confrontation with patriarchal domination which, like the contraband of colonial trade, is also exported to the territories of the empire. While Marlow is allowed to return to the center to reminisce about his adventure in colonial and patriarchal society, Rachel's female bildungsroman, that is, her recognition of the collusion between colonialism and patriarchy, ends in her death. Woolf's *Voyage* thwarts the master narrative tradition to which the story of Marlow belongs. Of the two methods, Woolf seems to come the closest to meeting Linda Alcoff's demand that "we . . . interrogate the bearing of our location and context on what it is we are saying, and this should be an explicit part of every serious discursive practice we engage in" (25).

PARODY AND THE CRITIQUE OF THE COLONIAL PROJECT: *BETWEEN THE ACTS*

Woolf's self-reflective approach to the colonial project is not limited only to her first novel but is pervasive among her writings. In particular, *Between the Acts,* her last novel, uses parody as an indirect method of criticizing British imperialism. Woolf's critique of the colonial project refuses to represent the voices of the colonized: instead, her insider position, at the center of empire, allows her to more aptly focus her criticism on the cultural and psychological manifestations of colonialism in the "mother country." Woolf's transnational feminist approach in her writings suggests that the participation of individuals in the worldwide struggle against tyranny does not require physical movement across national boundaries, but rather a deliberate and active awareness of the interrelatedness of exploitation and privilege which extend from center to empire. Woolf asserts in *Three Guineas* (1938) that "as a woman, I have no country. As a woman I want no country. As a woman my country is the whole world" (166). Here she acknowledges that Nazi fascism, on the one hand, and British patriarchy and colonialism, on the other, belong to the same continuum of power, and the threat of the former demands a self-reflexive appraisal of her own role in the latter. The praxis that follows this line of thinking is revealed in her writing. In *The Waves,* for example, Jane Marcus points out that there are 117 references to whiteness, symbolizing both class privilege and colonial domination as the by-product and material base, respectively, of English cultural ideology (144). "Virginia Woolf self-consciously creates here a literature of color, and that color is white, a literature written under the protection of the 'white arm' of imperialism and defining itself by the brown and black colonized peoples" (Marcus 143).

Woolf's approach to literary production and to intellectual life subscribes to, and prescribes, an interrogation of class privilege and the "missionization" of the lower classes of England by that society's intellectual elite. Her recommendation to her intellectual friends was that they "convert members of their own class to divest themselves of privilege, rather than become missionaries to the lower classes" (*Guineas* 154). In this way, Woolf demonstrates her belief in the power of insiders to effect change in the world around them by first changing themselves. Her lecture presented in 1940 to the Workers' Educational Association in Brighton (later published as "The Leaning Tower") evidences Woolf's belief that the intellectual elite should cultivate anticolonial, antifascist, anticlass, and antisexist positions within their own ranks and within the center of empire. This kind of praxis does not, however, express the inner feelings and ideology of the colonized. It calls attention to colonial subjugation and empire in such a way that the project of empire is weakened from the center, as in the instance of Portugal in the 1970s and the corollary collapse of Portuguese colonialism in Africa. Marcus suggests of Woolf's midcareer novel that

> The most powerful undertow in *The Waves* is class. The ruling-class characters define themselves as clean, free, and dominant against the dirt and ugly squalor of the masses. . . . Not only do the characters imagine their racial superiority by conjuring up Asia and Africa as the enemy whose assegais are poised against them, but they build their class superiority by hating and despising the working class. Rhoda is afraid of the "squalid" people in the Tube; Neville "cannot endure" that shopgirls should exist next to beautiful buildings; Susan sees country folk living like animals on a dungheap; and even Bernard composes little stories that betray his class and gender bias. (153)

In calling our attention to the class dynamic in *The Waves,* Marcus also forces us to engage in a mapping of Woolf's transnational strategy in the way in which she places classism, sexism, and racism on the same continuum with colonialism, and in doing so, speaks to both the internal and external contradictions of British ideology. The reader "overhears" snippets of conversation among the seven characters of *The Waves;* their comments about their "others" constitute a direct discourse of class and colonialist propaganda. This narrative technique is interrogated in her last novel, *Between the Acts,* which parodies British ideology and exposes the fragmentation and instability of art and intellectual life in the ongoing process of social change.

Structured as a play within a novel, *Between the Acts* attacks the class structure that affords the upper classes a lifestyle of leisure at the expense of the lower classes, a lifestyle which Woolf portrays as out of sync with a Europe at war. The first sentence of the novel finds her characters sitting in a large room on a summer's evening, "windows open to the garden," but the subject of their conversation is the cesspool (3). This symbol of dirt and decay contaminates Woolf's characters from the outset. Mrs. Haines, wife of a "gentleman farmer," has protruding eyes, "as if they saw something to gobble at in the gutter" (6). Her family's long history in the area could be proven by their "graves in the churchyard." The cesspool in question lies at a site "scarred by the Brittons; by the Romans; by the Elizabethan manor house; and by the plough . . . [during] the Napoleonic wars" (4). Mr. Bart Oliver, "of the Indian Civil Service, retired," remembers of his mother only that she was "stout" and "kept her tea-caddy locked" (5). His daughter-in-law, Isa, enters the room wearing a "faded dressing-gown" from tending to her ill son (4). Even her fantasies about Mrs. Haines's husband are "circled with a tangle of dirty duckweed," her "webbed feet . . . entangled by her husband, the stockbroker" (5). Their very conversation seems to disintegrate; sentences are started but not finished; random lines of Byron's poetry are misquoted; even Isa's daydreams are interrupted by Mrs. Haines's demands that "she recognize [her] existence" (6).

Not only is the class structure parodied as decadent, but so, too, is the colonial project which supports it. In "Voyaging Between Acts of Imperialism," Meg Albrinck notes that "Woolf presents imperialist behavior in mock-heroic fashion, thereby making it look ridiculous" (6). Bart Oliver's attempt to command his dog serves as an example:

> "Heel!" he bawled, "heel, you brute!" . . . they all turned to look at Sohrab the Afghan hound bounding and bouncing among the flowers.
>
> "Heel!" the old man bawled, as if he were commanding a regiment. It was impressive, to the nurses, the way an old boy of his age could still bawl and make a brute like that obey him. Back came the Afghan hound, sidling, apologetic. And as he cringed at the old man's

feet, a string was slipped over his collar; the noose that old Oliver always carried with him. (12)

The only subject Bart Oliver has left to dominate is his errant dog whose
name evokes his stint in the Indian colony.

Woolf makes it clear, through the characters of the novel, that the
continued existence of this egocentric, self-contained, historically focused lifestyle is pointless at best, and perhaps even doomed. The primary occupation of the residents of Pointz Hall, who have only been a
part of this village community for a mere 120 years, seems to be to fill
the leisure time provided through the labor of cooks, nursemaids, and
other domestic workers. Most of the summer, they spend looking at the
view which has not changed since it was described in "Figgis's Guide
Book (1833). . . . The Guide Book still told the truth. 1830 was true in
1939" (52). This view no longer satisfies them, however. "They stared at
the view, as if something might happen in one of those fields to relieve
them of the intolerable burden of sitting silent, doing nothing. . . . The
heat had increased. . . . All was sun now . . . flattened, silenced, stilled. . . .
The cows were motionless. . . . Old Mr. Oliver sighed profoundly . . .
Giles glared . . . Isabella felt prisoned" (65–66). The view, the summer,
the inactivity, the lifestyle have become a prison against which Giles,
Bart Oliver's stockbroker son, rages; the Pointz Hall family has become
"old fogies who sat and looked at views over coffee and cream while the
whole of Europe—over there—was . . . bristling with guns, poised with
planes" (53). While Giles seethes with frustration, his family chooses to
remain oblivious to the burgeoning war and the threat of invasion.

The major event of the summer is the annual pageant in which the
permanent residents of the village are enlisted for the entertainment of
the elite who spend their summers here. This play within the novel
spoofs English history, from the opening line "*England am I,*" and the
dramatization of the geological separation of the island from the main-
land during prehistory. The first act finds Queen Elizabeth ("Mrs. Clark
of the village shop . . . Eliza Clark, licensed to sell tobacco") bragging
about the "*sea faring men*" she commands who bring her "*oranges, in-
gots of silver, / Cargoes of diamonds, ducats of gold*" (84). She is unable
to enjoy the plunder of the non-Western world for long, though; the wind
dislodges her head dress, blows away her words, and Albert, "the village
idiot" (identified as such by "a stout black lady—Mrs. Elmhurst—who
came from a village ten miles distant where they, too, had an idiot"), appears on stage "picking and plucking" and "pinching" at the queen's

skirts (86). Between acts, the audience has tea in the barn still decorated from their celebration of "the Coronation" and inhabited by swallows who had come "[a]cross Africa, across France," to nest there (103).

Act 2 further foregrounds the colonial project of English history. Mabel Hopkins in a "grey satin robe (a bedspread)" emerges from the bushes (their dressing room). As the character "Reason," she justifies British economic dependence on the natural and human resources of the colonies:

> *Time, leaning on his sickle, stands amazed. While Commerce from her Cornucopia pours the mingled tribute of her different ores. In distant mines the savage sweats; and from the reluctant earth the painted pot is shaped. At my behest, the armed warrior lays his shield aside; the heathen leaves the Altar steaming with unholy sacrifice. The violet and the eglantine over the riven earth their flowers entwine. No longer fears the unwary wanderer the poisoned snake. And in the helmet, yellow bees their honey make.* (123)

Not only do the colonies provide riches, but they willingly lay their "*shield*[s] *aside*" and offer sacrifices to their deliverers. Even the flowers, snakes, and bees cooperate.

The next scene depicts the nineteenth century; Victoria, the "*White Queen,*" rules a "*Christian country, our Empire*" (162). Budge, the town drunk, has become a constable who directs traffic at "*Piccadilly Circus; at 'Yde Park Corner . . . the traffic of 'Er Majesty's Empire. The Shah of Persia; Sultan of Morocco; or it may be 'Er Majesty in person; or Cook's tourists; black men; white men; sailors, soldiers; crossing the ocean; to proclaim her Empire; all of 'em Obey the Rule of [his] truncheon*" (161–62). Our traffic cop is not only responsible for the direction of commerce throughout the colonies and within England, but also for the "*protection and direction . . . the purity and security of all Her Majesty's minions; in all parts of her dominions,*" including England's colonies in the British Isles (162). The "*redemption of the sinner,*" famine in Ireland, a turtle soup dinner, and the "*protection and correction*" of the "*natives of Peru*" are equally his responsibilities. The working class must be enlisted to this end:

> *The ruler of an Empire must keep his eye on the cot; spy too in the kitchen; drawing-room; library; wherever one or two, me and you, come together. Purity our watchword. . . . Let 'em sweat at the mines;*

cough at the looms; rightly endure their lot. That's the price of Empire; that's the white man's burden. And, I can tell you, to direct the traffic orderly, at 'Yde Park Corner, Piccadilly Circus, is a whole-time, white man's job. (163)

The play within the novel even takes a swipe at the missionary impulse and its part in the colonial project. The final scene of the "Victorian" act opens with two young lovers; Edgar's self-reflection leads Eleanor to admit that she, too, has *"longed to convert the heathen"* (166). Edgar then feels safe to offer her his mother's ring which she has passed on to him on the condition that he would give it only to a woman who was willing to share *"a lifetime in the African desert among the heathen."* This scene ends with a sumptuous picnic ("They did eat," remarks one of the audience) at which Edgar sings "Rule, Britannia."

Budge closes this act by implicating the family as the smallest unit whose responsibility it is to maintain British ideology. The *"gentlemen"* and *"ladies"* are sent home to the *"drawing-room and library,"* to the *"kitchen"* and *"nursary."* *"Mama"* is told to get her knitting and gather her children around her to read *"Sinbad the sailor"* or *"some simple tale from the Scriptures."* Women's job is clearly to reproduce the colonizing impulse, justified by the Bible, in the next generation: *"Let's build,"* Budge/the constable urges, *"a tower; with our flag on top"* (173). The family becomes the site of empire building, and women are portrayed as complicit in its construction. All classes, men and women, in the private arena, as well as the public, all British subjects must be enlisted to maintain England's global status.

We can read the final act of the play within the novel as Woolf's charge to artists, as the mirrors and creators of culture, to focus on the complicity of their own ranks in the creation and support of internal and external domination that is race- and gender-based. Miss La Trobe, who has written and directed the play, has created a carnivalesque history of England from prehistory to the Victorian era, when British colonialism was at its peak. Her critique shifts from this history to her audience, the English upper class (the proprietors of this enclave of summer homes), with the final act,"Present Time, Ourselves," a shift that they seem to dread. Giles, Dodge (a guest of the Olivers), and Isa are "damnably unhappy" (176).

The audience is "caught and caged; prisoners; watching a spectacle. Nothing happened." A record skips repeatedly on the record player as the restless audience becomes ever more uncomfortable, beginning to question just how a dramatist could hope to know them well enough to portray them on stage; still, nothing happens. The reader is left to wonder if the "spectacle" is only the play or if it is to be read as the audience, the characters, and the novel as well. It is not until Woolf reveals that the playwright's script says "After Vic . . . try ten mins. of present time" that we are assured that the audience are now the players (179). But Miss La Trobe is unhappy; the technique does not seem to be working: "Reality too strong . . . Curse 'em!" Then, after a brief, cathartic rain shower which causes not a single member of the audience to leave this outdoor arena, all the actors emerge carrying "Tin cans . . . Bedroom candlesticks . . . Old jars . . . the cheval glass from the Rectory . . . [a cracked] mirror . . . Anything that's bright enough to reflect [the audience]" (183). The gaze is turned from the players to the audience, but only "a nose . . . a skirt . . . trousers . . . perhaps a face" can be seen (184).

Miss La Trobe's vision of present-day England is a fragmented one. Confusion follows; Miss La Trobe fears she has failed. The local clergyman, for whose church the pageant was a fund-raising event, gets up to speak, but his comments on the meaning of the last act are blown away by the wind. Yet in the confusion, the audience reveals glimpses of self-recognition: "Did she mean, so to speak, something hidden, the unconscious as they call it? . . . Reflecting us . . . One feels such a fool, caught unprotected. . . . Mr. Streatfield . . . said she meant we all act . . . And if we're left asking questions, isn't it a failure, as a play? . . . Or was that, perhaps, what she meant?" (199-200).

Miss La Trobe cannot face the audience as they depart; she is unable to gauge the success or failure of her vision. At first she feels that she has given a gift to the world. Then the triumph fades: "Her gift meant nothing. . . . A failure . . . There was no longer view. . . . It was land merely." But she immediately begins to rethink her strategy, to imagine how she might have more successfully enacted her vision. She goes to the public house, and as she drinks and nods off, she imagines the first words of what will be her new play. The audience's confused response, Miss La Trobe's inability to assess that response, and her outsider status as an unattached female artist within both the indigenous community and the part-time summer residents of the village leave us with an ambiguous view of how effectively the arts can be used to incite social action.

Woolf's use of parody in *Between the Acts* pokes fun at the colonial mind-set of the economic elite. The female artist, a recurring figure in many of Woolf's novels, is evidence of a self-reflexive interrogation of the artist's role in social transformation and of the potential for artists to become themselves dictators of ideology. In "The Leaning Tower," Woolf advocates an insider politics that challenges the privileges of the British intellectual elite with a view toward a progressive transformation of that class for the benefit of the lower classes and the subjugated peoples of the empire. Woolf's commitment to social change in Britain was shaken by the threat of fascism which evoked her loyalty to nation and her sentimental attachment to intellectual life. Even her earlier assertion in *Three Guineas,* in which she denies membership in a nation, was called into question, since her privilege in taking such a stance was now threatened by the possibility of a fascist invasion.

Between the period of time when Woolf wrote *The Voyage Out* and the later works, *Three Guineas* (1938) and *Between the Acts* (1941), Woolf's "location" and that of her circle of leftist intellectual elite in England had begun to shift. Her first novel was written and submitted for publication before the beginning of World War I. By the time her last novel was completed (February 26, 1941), Hitler had invaded Austria, Poland, Norway, Denmark, Belgium, and Holland; Paris had fallen; the Woolfs' home in London had been damaged by bombing, and they had been forced to move their belongings and Hogarth Press to Monk's House, in Rodmell, in the country. Her sister Vanessa's eldest son, Julian, had died driving an ambulance in Spain, and despite Virginia's opposition, her pacifist husband, Leonard, had joined the Local Defence Volunteers, an armed resistance organization. Hitler's pogrom against the Jews and the threat of invasion of England had forced the Woolfs to plan a method of suicide, should the threat become reality—Leonard, as a Jew, and their community of leftist intellectuals would certainly have been in danger.

Woolf's capitulation to nationalism draws our attention to an African character in Raymond Williams's novel *Second Generation* (London, 1964), who remarks that nationalism "is in this sense like class. To have it, and to feel it, is the only way to end it. If you fail to claim it, or give it up too soon, you will merely be cheated, by other classes and other nations" (qtd. in Eagleton et al. 23). By the time she writes *Between the Acts,* Woolf is psychologically conscripted by British nationalism in the same way that the bodies of working-class young men are physically conscripted for service in defense of nation in time of war. According to Karen Schneider:

> [W]ar's psychic distress . . . seems also to have undermined her faith in
> the validity of her vision of an ultimate, unified reality underlying ap-
> parent fragmentation and, more important, faith in the efficacy of art to

effect social transformation. Most disheartening of all, the war eroded her faith in the possibility of any significant change in ways of seeing and being, a formidable blow to one whose life's work variously affirms the necessity of some liberating evolution in consciousness. (95)

Perhaps her self-confidence as an artist working for social change flagged near the end of her life. From the relatively "insider" position (as an organic intellectual seeking to transform the elite class) that Woolf occupied at the publication of *The Voyage Out,* from which she could critique Britain's patriarchal and colonial practices, she had moved to an "outsider" position—outside of the cultural center of London, the assumed hegemony of England, and outside of the organized leftist resistance embraced by her husband, nephew, and many of the male members of the Bloomsbury community, who viewed feminist concerns at such a time as "irrelevant."[6] By this time, the Bloomsbury group had shifted from a multifaceted analysis of oppression inclusive of antisexist and antiimperialist positions, to a relatively exclusive focus on national and antifascist concerns, demonstrating how the changing dynamics of global power relations influence struggle on the local level.

Virginia Woolf's greater commitment to nation, however, did not diminish her critique of the internal class contradictions of England or the external conditions of British colonialism. Likewise, the diminution of feminist concerns by her circle of intellectual leftists did not curtail her critique of British patriarchy. She acknowledges the alliance of colonialism and patriarchy in her frequent representation of British colonialists as males and turns to this alliance time and again in her other novels.

COMIC COLONIALS AND COMPLICIT INTELLECTUALS

Virginia Woolf's subversion of the bildungsroman as master narrative, her awareness of indigenous other and the thematic focus on their silence in her first novel, and her parodic use of upper-class English characters particularly in her last novel indicate a critique of empire that can be found in her other work as well. Those characters whose careers have been dedicated to the administration of the empire and those who romanticize the colonial experience form an unredeemed alliance in three of her most widely read novels, *Mrs. Dalloway* (1925), *To the Lighthouse* (1927), and *The Waves* (1931).

Woolf's use of parody is often directed toward the British civil service of the colonial empire. As *Mrs. Dalloway* opens, Peter Walsh has just returned from service in India to find that Clarissa, whom he once loved but who refused to marry him, has become what he both scorns and appreciates: the perfect hostess, wife of an administrative official in London. He visits with her as she prepares for a party that evening; Clarissa sews while Peter fondles his pocket knife. Clarissa, armed with a needle, and Peter, with an "old horn-handled knife which Clarissa could swear he had had these thirty years," do battle (65). On one level they are replaying an old personal drama of love, rejection, and regret, but on another level they are playing out the tension between the feminine keeper of the colonial Centre and the patriarchal servant in the empire.

Peter's surprise visit has taken Clarissa unaware, "like a Queen whose guards have fallen asleep and left her unprotected" (65). In response to her feeling that he sees her as "frivolous; empty-minded; a mere silly chatterbox," Clarissa admonishes him with "the things she [does]; her husband; [her daughter] Elizabeth" (65–66). Peter retaliates with "praise; his career at Oxford; his marriage . . . how he had loved; and altogether done his job" (66). He savors his "just-returned" status and the respect this status affords him as an expert on Indian affairs. Clarissa, who has been out selecting flowers for her party and who gives parties for heads of state, can be "gentle, generous-hearted" in "gratitude to her servants for helping her to be like this" (58). But Peter sees her life as a waste: "Here she is mending her dress; mending her dress as usual, he thought; here she's been sitting all the time I've been in India; mending her dress; playing about; going to parties" (61), while he radiates "journeys; rides; quarrels; adventures; bridge parties; love affairs; work; work, work!" (65).

While Clarissa's focus on the social aspects of life can be read variously either as Woolf's critique of the narrowness and restriction of women's roles, or as a celebration of women's culture, there seems to be little textual evidence that Peter functions as much more than a jilted lover who turns to the colonial service in India as a way to construct an identity. Clarissa describes him as having "the same queer look; the same check suit; a little out of the straight his face is, a little thinner, dryer" than when she last saw him (60). Richard Dalloway (Clarissa's husband), who is rather fond of Peter Walsh, remembers "how passionately Peter had been in love [with Clarissa]; been rejected; gone to India; come a cropper; made a mess of things" (161). Lady Bruton is glad that he has come back, "battered, unsuccessful, to their secure shores" (162). Sally Seton, a friend of Peter and Clarissa's when they were all young adults, describes him as "shrivelled-looking, but kinder" (285). Peter's self-concept is somewhat more romantic: "All India lay behind him; plains; mountains; epidemics of cholera; a district twice as big as Ireland; decisions he had come to alone" (72); he is "an adventurer, reckless . . . swift, daring, indeed (landed as he was last night from India) a romantic buccaneer" (80). But while his identity is constructed out of his colonial placement, he has an ambivalent attitude toward that position:

> Coming as he did from a respectable Anglo-Indian family which for at least three generations had administered the affairs of a continent (it's strange, he thought, what a sentiment I have about that, dis-liking India, and empire, and army as he did), there were moments when civilisation . . . seemed dear to him as a personal possession; moments of pride in butlers; chow dogs; girls in their security. (82)

He calls Indians "coolies" who refuse to use the wheelbarrows he ordered for them from England, and at the same time he expresses desire for a woman of color. He has returned to England to arrange for the divorce of a woman with whom he has fallen passionately in love; she is married to a major in the Indian Army, a representation of the Raj. But, while walking through the streets of London after his visit to Clarissa, he spies a young woman who becomes in his imagination "the very woman he had always had in mind; young, but stately; merry, but discreet; black, but enchanting . . . the red carnation he had seen her wear . . . making her lips red. . . . She was not worldly, like Clarissa; not rich, like Clarissa. Was she, he wondered . . . respectable?" (the stigma of race precipitates this concern) (79). It is this exoticized female other, whom he follows through the streets until she stops walking, looks in his direction without even seeing him, and enters her house, who inspires his self-description as a "romantic buccaneer" (80). Peter Walsh's self-construction contrasts with the limitations of Clarissa's female role. But like most of Woolf's colonial characters, Peter Walsh's concept of himself is to be questioned by the reader.

It is not only male characters, however, who epitomize the comic colonial. At Clarissa's party that evening we meet one character who is interested to talk with him only when she hears that Peter has been to Burma. Clarissa's Aunt Helena Parry had been in Burma in the 1860s and 1870s, and "her eyes (only one was glass) slowly deepened, became blue . . . at the mention of India, or even Ceylon" (271). At "past eighty" she is an "indomitable Englishwoman" whose colonial life had culminated in a book on orchids of Burma, of which Darwin himself had made mention. Her complete disregard of the humanity of colonial subjects and her disrespect for the land itself allowed her to paint "water-colour" pictures of orchids she had "uproot[ed]" while she was being carried through "mountain passes ... over solitary peaks" on the backs of "coolies" (271). Miss Parry's reinforcement of Peter Walsh's self-concept reveals, as well, her own romanticism of the colonial experience. In the character of Miss Parry, Woolf exposes the complicity of female subjects in the psychology of empire.

An older, more dissipated ex–colonial servant is a repeated guest at the Ramsays' summer home in *To the Lighthouse*. Augustus Carmichael seems to dislike Mrs. Ramsay, and has very little to say to other family members or guests, spending most of his time "basking with his yellow cat's eyes ajar, so that like a cat's they seemed to reflect the branches moving or the clouds passing, but to give no inkling of any inner thoughts or emotion whatsoever" (10). Mrs. Ramsay seems to feel sorry for him and explains to her other guests that he had "an affair at Oxford with some girl; an early marriage; poverty; going to India; translating a little poetry 'very beautifully, I believe,' being willing to teach the boys Persian or Hindustanee, but what really was the use of that?—and then lying, as they saw him, on the lawn" (10). It is her children who see him as a bit more sinister, calling their mother's attention to his use of laudanum, which stains his "milk white" beard and mustache yellow. In short, he seems to have little to recommend him as a houseguest, except to provide an outlet for Mr. Ramsay's magnanimity.

Mr. Ramsay, patriarch of the family and an academician, is respected by his peers and the ever changing string of graduate students who spend summers with the family, acting as his audience of admirers. His desire for fame and his concern for the longevity of his work seem mildly comic, yet tinged with something else by the end of the novel. In the final section, the family returns to the summer home after an absence of ten years and the deaths of Mrs. Ramsay and two of the eight Ramsay children. Mr. Ramsay finally forces his son James to take the rowboat trip over to the island on which the lighthouse stands, a trip that, as a child, James wanted but was always denied. Mr. Ramsay needs to mount this expedition as a way to gain something that he needs but is no longer provided. Gone is the wife who put aside her private self to care for him; gone are the graduate students he could impress with his grasp of the great philosophers. Lily Briscoe, an independent single female artist who also spent her summers with the family, now forty-four and "shrivelled slightly" in Mr. Ramsay's estimation, refuses to give him the sympathy he craves. Even Mr. Car-

michael, who had nothing to recommend him as a guest, has recently published a volume of his (forty-year-old) poems to modest success attributed
to a rising interest in poetry due to the war, and can no longer be seen as
totally dependent on Ramsay's generosity. Woolf stages this trip to the
lighthouse in such a way that the parallels to the voyage to colonize are
hard to ignore. Mr. Carmichael, the former colonial servant, and Lily
Briscoe, an artist who could potentially record the expedition, act as the
audience who remain at home to view the spectacle.

Mr. Ramsay sits in the middle of the boat, impatient until the sails
are raised and they are moving along quickly. The actual work of the
voyage, however, is provided by Macalister and Macalister's son, Scottish residents of the lighthouse island, who not only provide the labor to
operate the boat but also must provide stories about the death of several
local fishermen in a winter storm for Mr. Ramsay's vicarious enjoyment.
During the summers the family used to spend here, Mrs. Ramsay provided clothing, food, medicine, and emotional support during illnesses
for many of the permanent residents, maintaining a caretaker relationship. It is this relationship that Mr. Ramsay exploits for his own needs. A
"visit" to the island becomes a way to reconstruct Mr. Ramsay as a gen-
erous patriarch in the eyes of his adult children: the Centre using the other
to construct itself to itself. Woolf never allows the reader to become so
caught up in the journey that the sense of spectacle is lost. She interjects
short chapters which visit the "watchers" on shore who see the boat "in
the middle of the bay," then bobbing like a cork, then "swallowed up" by
the distance. The now grown Ramsay children, who had joined this expedition reluctantly, find their father's enthusiasm hard to resist: James
works the rudder; the speed and the mysteries of the sea hypnotize his
sister Cam; the pact between the two siblings to resist their father's
"tyranny . . . slackened a little" (165). Mr. Ramsay has long romanticized the life of the working-class permanent residents of the area, joining them occasionally for a "simple" dinner of cheese, meat, and bread at
a local public house. He dispenses the sandwiches he has brought for the
voyage: "Now he was happy, eating bread and cheese with these fishermen. He would have liked to live in a cottage and lounge about in the
harbour spitting with the other old men" (204). As the boat reaches the
lighthouse, he buttons his coat and puts on his hat:

> "Bring those parcels," he said, nodding his head at the things Nancy
> had done up for them to take to the Lighthouse. "The parcels for the
> Lighthouse men," he said. He rose and stood in the bow of the boat,

> very straight and tall, for all the world, James thought, as if he were saying, "There is no God," and Cam thought, as if he were leaping into space, and they both rose to follow him as he sprang, lightly like a young man, holding his parcel, on to the rock. (207)

Woolf constructs a scene that resonates with Columbus landing in the New World and creates in Mr. Ramsay a family patriarch who desperately needs the adulation of his subordinates and the appreciation of the working-class inhabitants of the lighthouse island. Woolf's Mr. Ramsay embodies the colonizing potential of the educated elite patriarchy to appropriate the other in the construction of itself.

The educated class is also Woolf's target in *The Waves* (1931). The novel follows a group of friends as they grow up and meet periodically to share their life experiences. The group comprises three men and three women and Percival, the usually absent character who becomes an Indian civil servant and around whom the group structures itself. They celebrate his triumphs as a schoolboy, meet to see him off on his move to India, and draw together to mourn his death there.

While Bernard is the writer who "makes up stories" about all the friends, it is Louis, whose father is a banker in Brisbane and who is marked as a colonial subject by his "unenviable body . . . large nose . . . thin lips . . . colonial accent," who perceives Percival's centrality (52–53). Bernard imagines Percival in India, righting an overturned bullock cart in five minutes by "applying the standards of the West by using the violent language that is natural to him" (136). For Bernard, "The Oriental problem is solved. He rides on; the multitude cluster round him, regarding him as if he were—what indeed he is—a God" (136). Jane Marcus comments on the mythmaking capacity of colonial literature as exposed through Bernard's "rewriting of the classic scene with a bullock cart in Kipling's *Kim* . . . the white man brings order and reason to the natives and is made a god" (158). Rhoda, who later commits suicide, also romanticizes Percival's colonial experience and its effect on the group:

> [H]e is like a stone fallen into a pond round which minnows swarm. Like minnows, we who had been shooting this way, that way, all shot round him when he came. Like minnows, conscious of the presence of a great stone, we undulate and eddy contentedly . . . the outermost parts of the earth—pale shadows on the utmost horizon, India for instance, rise into our purview. The world that had been shrivelled, rounds itself; remote provinces are fetched up out of darkness; we see

muddy roads, twisted jungle, swarms of men, and the vulture that feeds on some bloated carcass as within our scope, part of our proud and splendid province. (137)

Louis, the "best scholar at school," has gone "vaguely, to make money vaguely," in a "third class railway carriage," while the other men in the group go off to Oxford or Cambridge. It is he who understands that there is something false in this vision of Percival. Louis has embraced his own participation in the commerce of empire. He "like[s] to be asked to come to Mr. Burchard's private room and report on our commitments to China . . . hope[s] to inherit an arm-chair and a Turkey carpet" (168). "This is life . . . by dint of our united exertions we send ships to the remotest parts of the globe; replete with lavatories and gymnasiums. The weight of the world is on our shoulders. This is life" (169). It is perhaps because of his own participation in the colonial enterprise that he recognizes the collusion of the other members of the group:

> It is Percival, sitting silent . . . who makes us aware that these attempts to say, "I am this, I am that," which we make, coming together, like separated parts of one body and soul, are false. Something has been left out from fear . . . We have tried to accentuate differences . . . But there is a chain whirling round, round, in a steel-blue circle beneath. (137)

This "chain" could simply be an emotional bond the group shares, but because its anchor is the colonial civil servant, and because it is the colonial merchant who articulates its nature, the project of empire is implicated. Woolf gives Percival no voice in the novel, again allowing us to understand that while the colonial project is for some individuals one of adventure and conquest, it is, more importantly, the self-construction of the Centre.

Woolf will not allow us to read this enterprise as a positive bond, however. Percival dies in India, not as Bernard imagines him, galloping toward the enemy, death, "spear couched and . . . hair flying back like a young man's . . . unvanquished and unyielding," but falling off his "flea-bitten mare" when it trips (a reference, Marcus notes, to Forster's *Passage to India*). Woolf's discrepant versions of the colonial servant's death in the colony provide another warning against the writer's complicity in this project of self-construction. Woolf's resistance to speaking for the other and to the "othering" of colonized people leads her to a kind of postcolonial critique that interrogates these very acts. Through the characters of Peter Walsh and Miss Helena Parry in *Mrs. Dalloway,* Woolf ridicules the tendency of colonial civil servants and expatriated civilians to exoticize "blackness" and to romanticize the colonial experience. In *To the Lighthouse,* she uses allegory (the encounter of the English and the indigenous Scottish of the island) to mock the educated elite's appropriation of the colonial experience in the Third World as a means of self-construction. And in *The Waves,* through the intangible presence of Percival and through the act of signification in which she indicts master narratives (such as *Kim*) and repeats anticolonial literary sentiments (*Passage to India*), Woolf parodies vicarious adventurism and English literary tradition. Rather than give colonized people voice, which would have been an act of appropriation, Woolf leaves this responsibility to someone else, notably colonized people themselves.

One of the most obvious options for novelists writing on the colonial project is to allow the subaltern to speak for themselves. Such a novel would truly provide a dialogue between the polar agents of domination and subordination, in which the subordinates have hearts and minds and speaking tongues, as we will see in the following chapters.

Alcoff leaves us with a challenge concerning the act of speaking for others which we might apply to the writing and reading of the colonial novel: the bottom line, she says, is "[W]ill it enable the empowerment of oppressed peoples?" (29). While the novel may not be an art form as directly empowering as, for example, community-based theater, poetry, freedom songs, or direct social and political action, it must certainly have some critical impact on the complicity of those readers who are participants in the construction and maintenance of empire, on the one hand, and on their potential as agents of a liberatory praxis, on the other. Because Woolf does not allow her protagonist in *The Voyage Out* to return home, to the Centre, to tell of the "horror," the unknowable nature of the colonized other, and because she opts for an internal and often parodic critique of British colonialism at the center of empire in her other works, she resists the act of appropriation as a means for constructing the European "self." The threat of Nazi fascism stirred in Virginia Woolf nationalist sentiment but did not make her less critical of Britain's colonial ideology; instead, this threat may have evoked certain empathy for the peoples of the colonies upon whose land the English had encroached, much like an army of Fascists. For those of us who are concerned about those of and for whom we "speak" in the colonial discourse, Woolf provides possible models for investigating our own roles.

Her novels sustain an anticolonial, antinationalist, antipatriarchal, anti-Eurocentric, and anti-master narrative reading, and point us toward the engagement of political and narrative strategies which proliferate in transnational cultures and which point to the problems of "the relationship between feminism and nationalism, asking how feminist practices can exist outside certain master narratives" (Grewal and Kaplan 28). A discursive practice that attempts to expose the complicity of literature in the participation of colonialism and patriarchy needs as its custodian a critical reading practice sensitive to this important undertaking which Woolf and other women writers such as Zoë Wicomb champion in the pages of their work. Such a writing and reading practice advances a transnational feminism that acknowledges the scattered hegemonies that permeate discourses of gender.

NOTES

[1]In *Culture and Imperialism,* Said's analysis focuses on the relationship of Western literary culture (mainly the nineteenth- and twentieth-century novel) to the establishment and maintenance of Western imperialism. At the same time that he reveals the imperial project in modern Western canonical literature, he offers, for balance, ongoing efforts to decolonize it.

[2]Beer situates Woolf's writing at a historical juncture where the master narrative of evolutionary theory, especially Darwin's writing, was proving influential in biology, psychology, race theory, history, and other creative writing, such as that of Joseph Conrad and T. S. Eliot. While Conrad's Marlow and Darwin himself return successfully from their journeys into the unknown, Rachel does not. It is at the farthest point of her journey, the upriver excursion into primal nature, that Rachel and Terence acknowledge their love for each other and where, Beer notes, Rachel contracts the fever which finally kills her. While Beer acknowledges the presence of human beings in this jungle, in her reading the indigenous people seem not to be integral to Rachel's search for truth.

[3]Bayley claims that while many of the characters seem to be creating their own fictions, Rachel's inability to assimilate her role in heterosexual marriage can be read as her refusal to write her "story." Helen Ambrose, Rachel's aunt, must create the role of matron who guides the development of Rachel's feminine social skills, assuring her position in elite society. Susan and Arthur, also seasonal inhabitants of this "little England" in South America, must write their story as a newly engaged couple, acknowledging their social obligations and respective roles. Evelyn, the single woman, must invent a story that she can inhabit

when she returns to England unmarried. Rachel, however, dies rather than become a "character" in her own fiction. For Bayley, creating and living an acceptable social role is a journey that Rachel chooses not to take.

[4]The journey that Pamela Transue tracks is that of Woolf's developing feminism as it can be read in this novel through the parodic handling of the institutions of education, religion, and particularly, marriage, which, "even with so enlightened a partner as Terence, is too bound by tradition to accommodate the kind of change that Rachel's feminist vision demands" (33). Transue reads Rachel's death as a way to avoid the constricting role of heterosexual marriage.

[5]Harper provides a structuralist paradigm, tracking the narrative perspective beginning with a female voice which takes the reader inside the head of Rachel Vinrace and other female characters who wonder about women's role in the larger world. The narrative perspective then moves outward tentatively to encompass the self-examinations of the male characters, but retains as its central focus Rachel's exploration, until the narrative voice shifts from Rachel's fevered nightmares as she lies ill, to Terence's perception of her death as a kind of peace. *The Voyage Out* then becomes Rachel's voyage from her safe life with her aunts, as her father's housekeeper, toward the unknown realm of heterosexual love and marriage mandated by society. Rachel's imagined role in patriarchal marriage is, according to Harper, her "heart of darkness." Rachel's death is read as resistance to the role of wife. At the conclusion of the novel, Woolf shifts to a detached observer, St. John Hirst, to move the reader back to the comfort of polite English society, "the light and warmth, the movements of the hands, and the soft communicative voices" of the parlor at the hotel, a little England (Woolf 374). Harper's approach to the novel—that is, tracing how the shifts in narrative voice among the various British subjects also shifts the focus of the reader's attention—fails to break through the provincial trappings of colonial discourse where the boundaries of national consciousness mark the limit of human experience.

[6]This is an assessment that Patrcia Klindienst Joplin, in her essay titled "The Authority of Illusion: Feminism and Fascism in Virginia Woolf's *Between the Acts,"* credits to E. M. Forster, a member of the Bloomsbury group.

CHAPTER 3

Transnational Feminist Reading: The Case of *Cape Town*

The act of reading is far from a passive process by which the reader absorbs the text like a sponge. Yet I can imagine a reading of texts that closely approximates such passivity, particularly when the world of the text is alien to the reader. But a passive reading like this, no matter how alien its subject matter, is not exempt from the de rigueur demand of a transnational feminist reading practice. In the postmodern epoch, postcolonial theorists of many disciplines make us aware that master narratives and nationalism fail to represent the nature of social and political movements. A reading practice that is not an aggressive pursuit of understanding multiple subjectivities will tend to rely on a myopic, ethnocentric narrative, and will fail to capture the nuances of experience that national allegory often masks. In the final analysis, there is no such thing as a passive reading. A reading that is not passionately engaged in "joining" with various subjectivities (particularly those hitherto obscured by canonical formations) can, at best, be described as passive. But such a reading of a text, however, may not be passive at all, but rather the conservative embrace of master narrative that works against postmodernist perspectives and interpretations of aesthetic expression.

The first time I read South African feminist and author Zoë Wicomb's *You Can't Get Lost in Cape Town* (1987), it became clear that the novel required of me, a white, U.S., academic, feminist reader, a politically engaged reading practice. Initially, my entry into the text seemed deceptively simple. I, too, grew up as a female in a patriarchal society; I could share the female narrator's resentment of her father's expectations and the contradictory desire to do well in school, to make him proud. I remember the dissatisfaction with my maturing female body and the adolescent approach-avoidance attitude toward "boys" which the young Frieda expresses. But details of the novel prevented my easy identification with the narrator. Something as simple as Frieda's anticipation of a new school year on the last day of her summer holiday left me feeling "othered." Frieda looks around at the heat-dried "succulents spent and shrivelled in autumn" (23), yet she also notes that, at eighty degrees, "it is unusually cool for January" (21). The disjuncture represented by autumn in a different hemisphere provides only one example of the way in which the setting of the novel disallows my passive reading and demands a more aggressive pursuit of the "joining." However, the master narrative models of my Western education, even the canonized feminist reworkings of them, do not seem to provide an adequate framework to facilitate this effort.

For example, we might read the novel using the Western model of bildungsroman (or more specifically, a *künstlerroman*): the narrator, Frieda, a writer, matures, leaves South Africa for England, and eventually returns home with the idea that South Africa may be where she belongs. The most common (white, Western) feminist approaches to subverting the bildungsroman, such as Virginia Woolf's *The Voyage Out* and Kate Chopin's *The Awakening,* create a female protagonist who seemingly comes to understand what patriarchy expects of a woman, and they refuse to continue the journey, "choosing" death instead. Frieda, however, matures and negotiates gender expectations, neither accepting nor rejecting a "proper" feminine role. To the end of the novel, she continues to actively negotiate what it means to be a woman, and as importantly, what it means to be a "Coloured" South African.

Even my reference to *You Can't Get Lost in Cape Town* as a "novel" reveals an imposed sense of cohesiveness. In his analysis of this text, André Viola refers to the structure as a "cycle of stories," characterized by discrete episodes which share a "unity of place and singleness of focus" (Viola 231). Viola's structuralist approach compares *Cape Town* to James Joyce's *A Portrait of the Artist as a Young Man,* identifying in the development of the artist (in Frieda's case, the writer) "five stages, each concluded by a highly deceptive climax" (234). However, Viola's insistence upon comparing the text to master narratives, underscored by the title of his essay, "Zoë Wicomb's *You Can't Get Lost in Cape Town:* A Portrait of the Artist as a Young Coloured Girl," fails to recognize that Wicomb complicates the bildungsroman with the possibility that her main character has invented an imaginary life and denies the disruptive potential of reimagining literary conventions. A reading of *Cape Town* that situates it in the field of South African literature might be more responsible. While literature in South Africa is certainly informed by Western tradition, colonial languages and education being deeply integrated throughout the empire, a reading that uses as its only measurement Western canonical texts automatically places *Cape Town* outside of its historical, political, and social context, and as in the case of some readings of Woolf's *Voyage,* reifies master narratives.

Contextualizing a contemporary South African novel in its national literary tradition poses some problems for a transnational feminist reading practice, however. One project of transnational feminism is to free feminisms from narrow forms of nationalist discourse. The critique of British colonialism that I read in Virginia Woolf's *The Voyage Out,* for example, emerges from my use of her feminist essays as a guide for interpreting the silence which she creates around the indigenous women of the novel. Woolf's claim that as a woman she has no country, as a woman her country is the world, is an attempt to distance herself from a long national history of imperialism and to imagine alliances on the basis of gender. Likewise, Alice Walker's essay "My Father's Country Is the Poor" will serve in chapter 4 as a prime example of how she works against the narrow forms of black nationalism in the United States, itself a counterdiscourse, constructed solely on the basis of racial identity. As we will see, even the Pan-Africanist stance in her later novels resists the tendency to ignore patriarchal oppression for the sake of African solidarity.

But in South Africa, the notion of nation is even more complicated. As in the United States, the black liberation struggle of South Africa is a counternarrative to the white power structure and at the same time a master narrative of racial solidarity. The black liberation movement in South Africa elides differences of gender, religion, ethnicity, and socioeconomic class, a tendency which feminists such as Wicomb resist. However, the concept of "race" has been complicated by the apartheid structure that separated (physically and socially) black South Africans from "Coloured" South Africans, affording a certain level of "privilege" to the latter, a standard divide-and-conquer technique. The politically progressive "Coloured" community has claimed black identity and committed to a unified struggle. But South Africa's recent transition to majority rule, ending the reign of apartheid, signals an opportunity to complicate the nationalist narrative with ethnic and religious difference, gender-related issues, and gay and lesbian identities.

A master narrative approach to the reading of South African texts in the epoch of a postapartheid South Africa fosters a dependency upon long-established assumptions about identity formation and location as determined by racial policies under apartheid, on the one hand, and resistance to such policies by the national liberation movement, on the other. The term "postmodern" shares a common space with "postcolonial," and the application of the two terms to Third World literatures signals the disintegration of the master narrative of nationalist discourses which fail, at the present time, to account for all the fragments that colonialism leaves behind. Zoë Wicomb cites such a moment of disintegrating identity in the South African theater in her unpublished essay "Postcoloniality and Postmodernity: The Case of the Coloured in South Africa":[1]

> The resurgence of the term, Coloured, capitalised, without its prefix of *so-called* and without the disavowing scare-quotes earned during the period of revolutionary struggle when it was replaced by the word, black, has [much] in common with the condition of postmodernity: the successive adoption of names at various historical junctures; the failure of "coloured" to take on a fixed meaning; its shifting allegiances; and its typographic play of renaming whilst denying the act within an utterance that does not reveal capitalisation. (2)

Yet the strategic deployment of the term "Coloured" as a marker of postcolonial identity does not necessarily signal a politically progressive move. Wicomb's concern for the Cape coloureds of South Africa is, in part, motivated by their example as an instance of disintegrating identity vis-à-vis the "black" anti-apartheid movement and by their "shameful" support as a voting bloc supporting the Boer Party[2] platform during the first democratic elections on April 27, 1994:

> [T]he shame of [the vote] lies not only in what we have voted against —citizenship within a democratic constitution that ensures the protection of individual rights, the enshrinement of gay and lesbian rights, the abolition of censorship and blasphemy laws—but also in the amnesia with regard to the Nationalist Party's atrocities in maintaining Apartheid. (9)

The "we" in the above passage signifies Wicomb's membership in "Coloured" society, although this claiming is not her own but rather a category created by apartheid: Wicomb is a "Coloured" who identifies as black.[3] The example of Coloured identity and the disintegration of black nationalism which are Wicomb's concern also reveal the potential of postmodernity and postcoloniality to create new, reactionary forms of nationalism. As Wicomb puts it, "[W]ithin the new, exclusively coloured political organisations in the Cape, attempts at blurring differences of language, class and religion in the interest of an homogeneous ethnic group . . . defy the decentering thrust of postmodernism" ("Postcolonial-ity and Postmodernity" 2). Wicomb's valuing of the "decentering thrust of postmodernism" as a tactic of retaining the complexities of political and social identity in the postcolonial era provides a key to understand-ing identity construction in *Cape Town*. Even the structure of *Cape Town* demonstrates her postmodern tendency to destabilize the subject posi-tion. The text is a configuration of narrative fragments interrelated by a "Coloured" female narrator-protagonist, but otherwise disjunctured by the narrator-author's resistance to fixed locations. Such a text cannot be grasped by a passive or disinterested reading.

However, Wicomb's insistence that the conditions which gave rise to solidarity in black nationhood should not be forgotten must also shape a reading of her novel. Wicomb has been called a postprotest writer, "com-mitted to democratic ideals but refusing a single ideological stance" (Sicherman 111). Politically committed writing such as Wicomb's in postcolonial South Africa acknowledges its dependence on protest litera-ture, a counternarrative to colonialist representations which laid the groundwork for the institution of apartheid. The "protest" in "post-protest" is not a passive suffix paralyzed by an overdetermined prefix; nor is it a subordinate outdated appendage of South Africa's history. It acknowledges that the undoing of the symbolic features of apartheid South Africa has been no quick fix. The absence of de jure racial separa-tion has not resolved the hegemony of white privilege, nor the uneven distribution of material wealth in postapartheid South Africa. Further-more, a reading challenged by multiple subjectivities, and favoring frag-mentation over unification, may be vulnerable to a kind of bourgeois academic and aesthetic opportunism suggesting that the celebration of difference is more important than the material well-being of the masses. A valuing of the postmodern, multivoicedness of postcoloniality should not be divorced from real conditions created by the white power struc-ture. Hence, a reading of South African literature that aims to retain the social and political context of a text's creation would recognize that the protest model of South African literature is woven into postprotest writ-ings such as Wicomb's *Cape Town*.

Further complicating the concept of a "new" South Africa is the idea that there is some moment of epiphany when "old" becomes "new." The first majority election in 1994 was certainly a milestone in an ongoing struggle. But the dividing line between apartheid and postapartheid is slippery. Prior to 1994, black South Africans saw a loosening of restrictions on cultural production, and some formerly white-only educational institutions were opened to controlled numbers of "nonwhite" students. The ideas that the new contains the old and that the transition from one to the other does not take place linearly but in fits and starts are demonstrated in the literature of this period of transition. For instance, Zoë Wicomb's *You Can't Get Lost in Cape Town,* published in 1987, seven years prior to this momentous election, brings the "new" to bear upon the "old." Wicomb sets her novel in a South Africa still functioning under the apartheid system as she moves our reading of South African literature beyond the single focus on racial oppression in the protest model but not beyond the politics of a "new" South Africa. Protest is a fundamental aspect of South Africa's present and future; it is always already present in her narrative.

The goal of a transnational feminist reading practice is to imagine, through the vehicle of literature, cross-cultural alliances among women. Such a desire demands that the reader examine his or her own political assumptions. My initial naive approach to Wicomb's *Cape Town* assumed that a desire to understand the concerns of a South African female writer and our shared claim to feminism were sufficient preparation for imagining coalition. After being brought up short by textual references which cast me as "other," I realized that I could not ethically read this novel outside of its historical particularity. Reading Woolf's *Voyage Out* as anticolonial requires contrasting it to the exoticizing tendencies of colonialist literature. Likewise, Wicomb's postmodern exploration of the female subject builds upon the postprotest counternarrative which attempts to reveal what protest literature strategically obscures in its binary vision of the oppressed resisting the oppressor. Hence, an ethically responsible construction of postprotest literature might begin by uncovering what it works against.

". . . LIKE LIVING ON SHIFTING SANDS"[4]: PROTEST LITERATURE IN SOUTH AFRICA

A thorough examination of South African literature would recognize the colonialist writings that protest literature challenges. Titles of early English-language "ancestral novels" echo colonialist prejudices and concerns: *Makana: or, the Land of the Savages* (1832); *Jasper Lyle: A Tale of Kaffirland* (1852); *George Linten: or, the First Years of an En-*

glish Colony (1876); and *The Settler and the Savage* (1877). Sarah Christie, Geoffrey Hutchings, and Don Maclennan, coauthors of *Perspectives on South African Fiction,* suggest that early white South African writers who employed the novel form adopted English master narrative styles such as the pastoral, romance, and realism, and adapted them to the South African setting. Yet such classifications, which grow out of a literary tradition at the heart of the colonial project, do not sufficiently address the hegemonic place of race in South Africa.

What we now know as the state of South Africa began as a settler colony, established by the Dutch East India Company at the Cape in 1652 as a way station for eastbound traders. Dutch settlers displaced the indigenous Khoi,[5] then spread inland as "Trek-Boers," seeing themselves as early pioneers settling a savage land. As the Boer population increased, more and more farmland was required. Control of the Cape transferred from Dutch to British hands as a result of the Anglo-French wars of 1793–1815. Dutch descendants resisted British authority until they were granted "independence" from the British colonial administration in 1910. Caught in a litany of struggle between the two settler populations, the English and the Dutch, were numerous indigenous African cultural groups who suffered displacement and enslavement, and who sometimes fought back violently and were subsequently suppressed. Since the 1910 Act of Union until the granting of majority rule in 1994, the business of what to do with the African population was a major concern of the white power structure. All aspects of the lives of "nonwhite" inhabitants were subject to legislation: where they lived and worked, what they could and could not publish or say publicly, even what constituted immorality. The colonial settlers also legislated terms upon which the indigenous population surrendered to the white authorities the very land upon which they had lived for generations; white economic development took priority over African humanity. The structure of apartheid ("apartness") was built upon racial classifications which define Africans in negative terms. According to the Population Registration Act of 1950, "whites" are Afrikaans-speaking, English-speaking, or immigrants (usually identifying with English-speaking whites); "nonwhites" are comprised of "Coloureds," "Asiatics," and "Bantu." The Immorality Act (1949), pass laws, and land acts served to ensure separation of "whites" from "nonwhites" and to severely punish transgressors.

Given the implications of racial identity in such a setting, South African author and critic Lewis Nkosi comments in his critique of African literature, *Tasks and Masks* (1981), that with very few exceptions the literature of Southern Africa is wholly concerned with the theme of struggle and conflict—conflict between the white conquerors and the conquered blacks, between white masters and black servitors, between the village and the city. In particular, if South African literature seems unable to contemplate any kind of human action without first attempting to locate it within a precise social framework of racial conflict it is merely because very often colour differences provide the ultimate symbols which stand for those larger antagonisms which Southern African writers have always considered it their proper business to explain. . . . [W]hether written by white or by blacks the literature of Southern Africa is committed to the notion that certain 'tasks' are the legitimate function of socially responsible writers. Protest, commitment, explanation: Southern African readers and critics expect these qualities of their authors. (76)

From its inception, the field of protest literature gives voice to a culture of resistance. The first black novel, *Mhudi* (1922), by Sol Plaatje, responds to the Land Act of 1913 which displaced the indigenous people from their farming and grazing lands and paved the way for the apartheid structure. Zoë Wicomb notes that Plaatje's literary prediction of the decimation wrought by this system and his appeal to black nationhood utilize the form of a traditional, orally transmitted folktale as an analogy ("Nation" 16). Later protest writers, however, "borrow their models from American literature, primarily that of black Americans" (Nkosi, *Tasks and Masks* 81). The appropriation of an African American literary model by South African authors confirms the hegemonic position of racial relations under apartheid, since it is race antagonism that has been the preoccupation of black American literature, and the African American protest model seems to be a pervasive and healthy response to racial oppression.

Nkosi's critical appraisal of South African writers such as Enver Carim, Nadine Gordimer, Alex La Guma, and Bessie Head favors "protest, commitment and explanation" as the appropriate focus of South African literature. Enver Carim's *A Dream Deferred* (1973), for example, provides for Nkosi "some grisly insights into the dialectical relationship between the conqueror and the conquered; and it is this relationship between the white rulers and their black subjects, the resultant corruption of one and the dehumanisation of the other, which absorbs and exhausts the energies of the South African writer" (*Tasks and Masks* 80).

Common themes echo through much of South Africa's protest literature. In his 1964 play *The Rhythm of Violence,* Nkosi utilizes the student

protest movement as a vehicle for dramatizing organized militant resistance and exposing brutal repression on the part of the police. Two
groups of characters enact the racial conflict. The play opens with a conversation between two machine gun–toting Boer policemen in the waiting room of Johannesburg city hall. Their presence is juxtaposed with an
African freedom rally taking place outside. The physical location of the
two groups immediately establishes the binary of race relations in the
play. These two representatives of the white power structure are concerned with how best to contain the hated black freedom movement and
still retain their own sense of "humanity." This internal discord, inherent
in the psyche of the colonizer, serves as instance of diametrical conflict
in protest literature. The author attempts to subvert the binary tendencies
of the protest model by representing the student movement as a potential
site of racial integration and political solidarity. One objective of protest
literature is to overthrow the relations of antagonism that have made it
necessary. With the introduction of white student activists, particularly
the pivotal role played by the Afrikaner character Sarie, Nkosi weaves together the personal and political of apartheid South Africa using interracial relations as his vehicle. But his staging and the political affinity of
the student activists retain an oppressor-oppressed duality.

In Nkosi's novel *Mating Birds* (1986), the suppression of student activism prefigures concern for what happens to the dispossessed black
youth of South Africa. The narrator, Ndi, has been expelled from the University of Natal for protesting segregated classrooms and the kind of
Afrikaner scholarship that teaches that "before the white man came there
was no African history to speak of in this darkest of the Dark Continents.
Whether we like it or not, African history commences with the arrival on
African soil of the first white man" (104). Because Ndi lacks a student pass
due to the expulsion, and is unable to obtain a work pass, he seeks out the
safest place to spend his days, the "blacks only" side of the Durban beach
which is "safe" because the presence of foreign tourists tends to curtail the
public display of the brutal methods of the South African police.

In order to symbolize the "dehumanization" of the indigenous population resulting from the malevolent polices of the South African government, Nkosi uses interracial relations at their most intimate level in this
novel. The first-person narrator is convicted of rape and sentenced to
hang for breaching the Immorality Act, which forbids sexual contact between the races. The narrator's predicament resembles that of Bigger
Thomas, who is also executed for his sexual transgressions, in the proto-
typical U.S. protest novel, *Native Son* (1940) by Richard Wright. The

public beach in *Mating Birds* replicates the racial divide of South African society: the two main subjects face each other from opposite sides of the color line. Their publicly shared, yet separate, location becomes a place of sexual intrigue. In the private sphere, the bedroom of the white subject (Veronica), mutual sexual desire is enacted. With the reimposition of the public, as their tryst is discovered by her Boer friends, sexual desire degenerates into racial betrayal through her accusation of rape. The public imposition of apartheid upon the private desires of the subjects exacts the betrayal of the black narrator by his white lover, and reflects the author's claim that the "relationship between the white rulers and their black subjects . . . [results in the] corruption of one and the dehumanisation of the other" (*Tasks and Masks* 80).

But while protest literature in Nkosi's hands eloquently demonstrates the insidious link that "apartness" constructs across racial classifications, it constructs race as the only basis for oppression in South Africa. A feminist reader might ask, "Where are the women in this version of protest?" In Nkosi's *Rhythm,* female student activists are a supporting cast, concerned with providing food and beer for the political meeting, and functioning as objects of sexual banter among the men. The only woman who is minimally developed is Sarie, and we are led to believe, at the conclusion of the play, that she will inadvertently betray the students. The female characters are not fully developed in Nkosi's novel *Mating Birds* either. In his reminiscences of her, the narrator's mother is constructed as a passive victim of the apartheid policies. Land "reform" acts have claimed ancestral land and have forced her to move into the city; pass laws restrict her residence to the townships and limit employment opportunities, forcing her into one of the more lucrative, though illegal, occupations available to African women, brewing and selling homemade beer. Likewise, Veronica appears only as the first-person narrator's story constructs her: an object of sexual desire. She never speaks except to betray him, and Nkosi offers little to suggest that the narrator's version of events is to be read as anything but the unequivocal truth.

Just as Lewis Nkosi's literary vision seems limited to a binary construction of race relations and fails to develop any gender concerns, Bessie Head, one of the few widely published female writers of color in South Africa, focuses on the effects of South African apartheid on the black man in her first novel, *When Rain Clouds Gather* (1969). *Rain Clouds* centers around a black South African, Makhaya, who has spent some time in jail and climbs a barbed wire fence to escape into Botswana. The rural village to which he flees seems to offer the "illusion of freedom" from the chaos of life as a black man in urban South Africa

(7). The pastoral landscape and simple lifestyle provide a kind of peace for a community of exiles of various types, several from difficult personal situations in other parts of Botswana, one a refugee from an emotionless, middle-class English family. While Makhaya's escape testifies to the difficulty of life in South Africa, Head does not romanticize subsistence farming in rural Botswana. The protagonist's adjustment from urban to rural life and his alienation in exile are eased only somewhat by the communal interdependence that results from drought and the hard labor of cooperative agriculture.

The dearth of full-blown female characters in this early novel by Head and in the body of protest writing described thus far is attenuated somewhat by Miriam Tlali. Tlali's work can be called "protest" in terms of both content and style. Like Nkosi, she addresses the social and economic effects of a politics of racial domination. And unlike the approach of a postprotest writer like Zoë Wicomb, whose "novel" employs discursive strategies that suggest, insinuate, and open up spaces for negotiated readings, Tlali's approach is straightforward and explanatory. She constructs her first novel, *Muriel at Metropolitan,* completed in 1969 and banned until its publication in abbreviated and censored form in 1975, as highly autobiographical. Tlali presents the day-to-day life of Muriel, a black typist at Metropolitan Radio, a Johannesburg appliance store, and examines the intersecting sites of race and class oppression from the perspective of a female protagonist. *Muriel at Metropolitan* reveals the economic effects of apartheid by showing how the dubious system of "hire purchase" agreements further indebts and impoverishes the black population. The scenario Tlali creates would not be unfamiliar to the poor in any capitalist system, since the time-payment system is a pervasive practice serving to ensure economic dependence. Unlike Nkosi's approach of radical integrationism, Tlali's work seems concerned only with life within the black community. *Muriel at Metropolitan* echoes themes identifiable with the South African protest movement. Tlali's references to incarcerated leaders on Robben Island, the disintegration of the African family resulting from the policies of labor migration, loss of land and displacement of the black population due to land reform policies, and the call for collective action on the part of the black proletariat are signatures of the lived experience of a person of color in South Africa and define its protest literature.

A critique of apartheid is also articulated in protest literature written by white South Africans. Nadine Gordimer, for example, focuses on what seems appropriate: white complicity. Critic Robin Visel notes, "Gordimer's white South African women are in a sense outside the brutal pact between the male colonizer and the male colonized. But Gordimer refuses to let the white heroine off the hook as a fellow victim; she insists not on woman's passivity, but on her shared responsibility, her collusion in racism" (34). Like Lewis Nkosi's writing, a frequent concern throughout Gordimer's fiction is the taboo of black-white relations under apartheid. In her work, white South Africa is often associated with dryness, sterility, and death, while for her white heroines, " 'blackness' is linked to sex, sensuality and imagination" (Visel 34); her tendency to sexualize black characters has been, at times, soundly criticized. From her early concern for the political responsibility of aesthetics in *The Late Bourgeois World* (1966), the ideological framework that Gordimer consistently brings to bear upon the South African situation is Marxism. In contrast to the above-mentioned examples of protest literature which utilize realist forms, Gordimer offers a more experimental style while still addressing themes of resistance.

Gordimer's style moves from modern Western literary forms like the bildungsroman in her earlier novels to a more postmodern narrative in her later work. Many critics identify *Burger's Daughter* (1979) as a point of stylistic transition with its "shift from the centrality of the subjective and individual to include South Africa in its various highly contested sets of relations, attitudes and voices" (King 6). For example, the novel includes actual police reports and "genuine black African student tracts, the mixing of the real with the imaginary" (King 6–7). But at its heart, *Burger's Daughter* is a bildungsroman concerned with Rosa Burger's struggle to find her own identity. Rosa has been raised in a socialist family and, upon the death of her parents, must work out her own place in the South African political landscape. Even the title "announces that at the novel's core there is a Freudian family saga" (King 7). Rosa's voluntary exile ends when she embraces the work of the ANC; *Burger's Daughter* imagines a place in South African protest for a white activist and so complements the protest literature written by South African writers of color.

But the project of constructing a literary history for Wicomb's 1987 novel defies this linear notion of literary development. South African protest literature does not transform into postprotest with any particular event in the struggle for independence. Lewis Nkosi's *Mating Birds* was published in 1989, for example, two years after Wicomb's *Cape Town,* yet his novel seems to be clearly consumed with the hegemony of racial oppression. Complicating the landscape of South African literary development are the flow of writers out of South Africa and the difficulties of publishing within the country under apartheid. Nkosi, Head, and

Wicomb have written and published from locations of exile/expatriation. While Nkosi's play and novel do not address exile, Head's later novels and Wicomb's *Cape Town* bring this experience, as well as their "Coloured" identity, to bear to disrupt the protest form. For example, Miriam Tlali's 1989 collection *Soweto Stories* was written while she lived in South Africa, accounting perhaps for its stylistic similarity to the protest form—daily life in the townships, even in a changing South Africa, requires daily, direct resistance. Yet in this recent collection Tlali troubles the hegemony of race issues in protest literature with a critique of black patriarchy.

A reading practice concerned with contextualizing the work of a South African female writer of color must be cognizant that literary production in South Africa has been hampered by the effects of apartheid. Published works by South African women of color comprise a fairly small body of work. The daily lived experience of apartheid limits access to education and the material resources that facilitate the production of literature. Apartheid has brutally limited blacks' access to education, directly through withholding funding, and indirectly by making daily survival so difficult. Cultural banning, which restricted any work that was openly critical of the Boer government, has been particularly successful in discouraging the novel form. Many political writers living in South Africa have had to seek publishers outside of the country, often secretly, and poetry and short stories are easier to camouflage than book-length manuscripts. Because at present there are relatively few published black South African writers, I offer Miriam Tlali's *Soweto Stories* and Bessie Head's *Maru* (1972) and *A Question of Power* (1974) as available examples to which we might turn as a source of the issues raised in postprotest literature by South African female authors and which might inform a reading of *You Can't Get Lost in Cape Town*. Additionally, the post-protest visions of white South African authors whose creative production has not been limited in the same way as that of black South Africans may provide an interesting contrast.

TROUBLING RACIAL HEGEMONY: "POST"-PROTEST LITERATURE

The short fiction collected in Miriam Tlali's *Soweto Stories* works against the "orthodox" anti-apartheid position which, while "celebrating the political activism of women, [claims] that the gender issue ought to be subsumed by the national liberation struggle" (Wicomb, "To Hear"

37). Tlali's short stories are peopled with female characters who resist apartheid as gendered beings. We see the migrant labor camps through the eyes of a wife who has had to leave her children and travel 150 miles from the "native reserve" to visit her husband to " 'fetch' another child" (44). After her husband's arrest under the pass law, she is helped by strange women at the camp as she gives birth to a new child, far from her home and family support. In another story, a petit bourgeois man from Soweto is attacked and his car is stolen by *tsotsis;*[6] women flock out of the surrounding houses, blowing whistles and sending out the alarm; female community action proves the most effective way to deal with the errant youth.

In this collection, Tlali reveals the intersections of black patriarchy and racial oppression under apartheid. Displacement from ancestral lands leaves women caught in the conflict between rural and urban life, and traditional and modern culture. In several of her stories, overcrowding, housing restrictions, assignment to specified areas, alcoholism, and unemployment work against traditional support networks of extended family and male financial responsibility. For Paballo, the protagonist in "Mm'a-Lithoto," additional pregnancies are no longer a joy but a burden. The traditionally male-headed household means that it is her husband, Musi, who "owns" the home in the township; when his extended family are displaced from their farm, it is his responsibility to share his scant space. When her husband's expectations that she wait on his family, the crowded living conditions, and her advancing pregnancy become too much for Paballo, her only alternative is to take her child and leave. But her own extended family are also restricted to the townships; they have no room for her. Tlali's stories reveal that the support networks that were available to women within traditional, patriarchal rural life are rendered ineffective by city life; Paballo's male family members who would mediate such marital disputes, fining the husband in oxen for his failure to provide suitable housing for his wife, are powerless in the black urban township.

Tlali's women also suffer from modern sexism, intensified by the effects of apartheid. Sexual abuse on trains, extremely overcrowded by the politics of segregation, is so common that the women do not even need to name it to know they share the experience. Yet the white-only trains which run on parallel tracks are never full; everyone gets a seat. In "Devil at Dead End," negotiations required of a black female passenger to obtain a second-class train ticket so that she will have a place to rest on her overnight journey, leave her vulnerable to the white ticket taker's sexual lust.

Both *Muriel at Metropolitan* and *Soweto Stories,* Tlali's earliest and latest published literature, respectively, share certain stylistic characteristics. Rather than the figurative language and literary tropes often identified with *l'art pour l'art,* we find unambiguous statements and calls to action. Both works frequently use the modifier "so-called" preceding terms like "coloured," "mine boys," "delivery-boys," and "boss-boy," throwing into question the legitimacy of the discourse of apartheid. Both works satisfy the "tasks," offered by Lewis Nkosi, of socially responsible literature: protest, commitment, and explanation. But Tlali's style has changed. *Soweto Stories* weaves together many and varied narrative voices, women of all ages and even men speak from its pages. This collection moves beyond the more straightforward autobiographical protest fiction of *Muriel at Metropolitan,* written twenty years before, by decentering the subject position, displacing it from an easy one-to-one correlation with the author. Furthermore, Tlali's use of footnotes and parenthetical explication in *Soweto Stories* might be read as a discursive strategy creating a more polemic feel and an appeal to a non–South African readership.[7] The meaning of characters' African names is translated; publication banning, border-crossing procedures, and university policies are explained. A consciously political reader might look to the context of the text's production to appreciate such authorial strategies. Between the time that Tlali wrote *Muriel at Metropolitan* and *Soweto Stories,* she had left southern Africa for the first time, visited the Iowa Writing Program in 1978, and become aware of a small but expanding international readership. Because the anti-apartheid movement has been, in part, carried out on a global stage, with local and international activists requesting economic sanctions against the nationalist government in support of majority rule in South Africa, the style of Tlali's later work might well be read as an appeal for transnational feminist protest.

Just as Miriam Tlali renders problematic the master narrative of South African protest literature on the basis of gender, her contemporary, Bessie Head, complicates the racial politics of this form. Born in Pietermaritzburg Mental Hospital in Natal, Head was the daughter of a white upper-class woman who was judged insane and committed to the mental hospital while pregnant. Her father was a black stable worker for her mother's family, and Head knew even less about him than she did about her mother, Bessie, after whom she was named. Sent immediately to a foster home, to English mission school at the age of thirteen, and then to train as a teacher, Head was a first-generation biracial child who grew up outside of the Cape Town "Coloured" community. She was one of the group of South African writers referred to as the *Drum* (magazine) school, and she lived in Cape Town's District Six for three and a half years while in her twenties. But the mere assignment of the classification "Coloured" did not buy her entry into the Afrikaans-speaking Cape "Coloured" community. "Coloured" identity in South Africa suggests images of the discursive stereotype of the tragic mulatto: a hybrid existing in the interstices of racial identity. To be "Coloured" is to be homeless (if you do not live in Cape Town), and for Bessie Head, homelessness was intensified by her exile in Botswana. Leaving marriage, family, and job, she left South Africa with her only son on a one-way, no-return exit visa and began a fifteen-year period of refugee status, until she was finally granted Botswana citizenship in 1979. It is the investigation of racial and geographic rootlessness in Head's novels which create gaps in what might seem like a seamless South African narrative of binary racial antagonism.

Head, like other *Drum* writers, was "educated, articulate, and well read" (MacKenzie xiv), but her regular contributions differed from theirs stylistically. Most *Drum* writers' work tended to be journalistic and overtly political; Head's more personal, often autobiographical style and avoidance of directly political topics foreshadowed the tone of her later novels. Like Head's earlier novel, *When Rain Clouds Gather, Maru* (1972) falls within the protest literature tradition but at the same time hints at the identity fragmentation which marks *A Question of Power* (1974) as a postprotest, postmodern novel.

Unlike *Rain Clouds* and *A Question of Power,* Head's second novel, *Maru,* does not have a South African protagonist, yet it takes up homelessness and the ambiguity of "Coloured" identity in the central character, Margaret Cadmore. Margaret was raised, as an "experiment," by an English missionary woman who took her as a newborn (her mother having died in childbirth), gave the child her own name, and raised her in the mission school. Young Margaret seemed to have "a big hole" in her identity because "she was never able to say: 'I am this or that. My parents are this or that' " (15). Yet race was imposed: "There was no one in later life who did not hesitate to tell her that she was a Bushman, mixed breed, half breed, low breed or bastard" (16–17). Margaret is a Masarwa, an ethnic group that functions as the servant class for the African people in the busy administrative village where Margaret is hired to teach. Her ethnic identity is obscured by her adopted English name, and upon arrival in the village, her appearance marks her as "Coloured" South African. With the abuse, discrimination, and alienation that Margaret suffers when she publicly claims her Masarwa identity, Head demonstrates a caste system which collapses rural/urban conflict, race/ethnicity, and socioeconomic class, a caste system that could equally well describe South Africa under apartheid.

While her first two novels complicate the racial politics of an anti-apartheid literary tradition, Head's third novel, *A Question of Power,* is the most highly autobiographical of her novels, yet it takes identity fragmentation to its limit. The novel centers around a "Coloured" protagonist, Elizabeth, who has "lived on the edge of South Africa's life" and leaves on a one-way visa to teach in rural Botswana (18). The bulk of the novel centers around Elizabeth's mental breakdown; she is caught in an internal struggle between two forces in male form who might be read as a Ghandi-like spiritualist (with a Medusa alter ego) and an African nationalist (and insatiable womanizer). The good versus evil allegory is racially marked by the white robes of the spiritualist and the very dark complexion of the nationalist. Through these two inner "demons," Elizabeth must sort out her feelings of not being a "proper African" as a mixed-race person with no clear sense of national identity. Elizabeth's location as a "Coloured" and her condition of exile offer us another vantage point from which to examine the effects of the experience of South African apartheid. But unlike protest writers whose focus continues to be determined by day-to-day struggle against apartheid, Head's *A Question of Power* suggests a more personal focus and potential resolution. The novel ends with Elizabeth's mental reintegration and her embrace of the communal farming project run by local women. The Cape gooseberry bush that they have transplanted to rural Botswana flourishes.

The discursive fracture of the hegemonic protest narrative by Head's insistence upon multiple subject positions and her correlation of mixed racial identity with the condition of exile will provide a literary context for reading the expatriation of Wicomb's "Coloured" protagonist. Likewise, the postprotest visions created by widely read authors Nadine Gordimer and J. M. Coetzee might provide insight into the postapartheid concerns of white writers, and a source of comparison for Wicomb's final vision in *Cape Town.*

In recent years, as it became apparent that majority rule in South Africa was inevitable, and particularly following the 1976 Soweto uprising, concern for what shape such a transition might take and what its effects might be on the minority population has been taken up in the fiction of Gordimer and other white South African writers. In his analysis of this literary trend, critic Bernth Lindfors refers to Gordimer's futuristic novel of South Africa, *July's People* (1981), and J. M. Coetzee's allegorical

Waiting for the Barbarians (1980) as "apocalyptic." Gordimer's novel is
set during an ongoing revolution; the Smales family have become dependent upon July, their former "houseboy," for survival. Gordimer focuses
on the liberal white family's dilemma of being caught between different
factions of the majority population struggling for control, yet her vision
of post-"apocalypse" African life seems unsympathetic to black South
Africans. Gordimer "concentrates mainly on the dirt, offering clinical
descriptions of unhygienic conditions and unhealthy practices that make
the Africans we see look obdurately backward. The coldness of
Gordimer's view of Africa is disturbing . . . the future is memorable prin-
cipally for its obsession with uncleanliness" (Lindfors 201–2). Lindfors
moves from the futuristic *July's People* to the "apocalypse" of Coetzee's
Waiting for the Barbarians, reading the last part of *Barbarians* as another kind of prediction for South Africa. The collapse of the frontier set-
tlement finds the "human debris of empire [waiting] for the barbarians to
arrive and obliterate their civilization" (203). While Lindfors notes that
Coetzee's choice of allegory allows this ending to be read as the death
throes of any "alien civilization" replaced through bloody revolution, he
concludes by suggesting that, especially coming so quickly after Soweto,
Coetzee may have written the novel "to remind his countrymen that
someday soon the end will come, just as it has come to other peoples
elsewhere in the world throughout recorded time" (203).

Although not necessarily chronological, my arrangement of South
African writers suggests an increasingly fractured South African narrative—Nkosi by Tlali's feminism, Tlali and Nkosi by Head's racial ambiguity. Gordimer and Coetzee disrupt the realist narrative with their
postmodern stylistics. Yet futuristic imaginings and apocalyptic allegories can aestheticize and universalize the literary political landscape to
the point that the reader no longer knows who the enemy is. A transnational feminist reading practice demands that we resist a relativism that
allows texts to be read as simply individual expression. Literature can
provide one arena for doing the kind of comparative political work demanded of transnational feminism. The global oppression of women
must be investigated as taking place in multiple sites which are both discrete and overlapping. A Western/First World reader who wants to imagine solidarity with South African women, utilizing a postmodern text
such as *You Can't Get Lost in Cape Town,* would negotiate the conditions that give rise to difference at the same time as he or she desires the
"joining."

A NOVEL FOR A NEW SOUTH AFRICA

Rather than uncritically embrace as integral to postcolonial literature postmodernism's tendency to break down subject-object and self-other binaries inherent in colonial representations and strategically adopted in nationalisms, a transnational feminist reader needs to look to a theory of subject construction that is not unitary or essentializing but is "heterogeneous as well as political, destroys binarism, and is inclusive. This subject provides a constant critique of nationalist and even insurgent agendas, of power relations that structure global economic flows, and will never be complete" (Grewal, "Autobiographic Subjects" 234). At the same time, transnational feminism wants to retain the conditions of that subject's emergence.

The South African master narrative of protest literature, with its binary construction of racial politics, has tended to obscure the multiple subject positions of South African women. But a postmodern aesthetic practice as an antidote should not erase the protest foundation from which postprotest literature springs. It was author James Baldwin who raised, in the arena of African American literature, the issue of aesthetic possibility in literature that is overtly political, a debate which is currently ongoing among South African writers and critics. According to Richard Barksdale and Keneth Kinnamon, Baldwin worried, "Does protest of any kind impair the artistic merit of a novel, a poem, or a short story?" Baldwin argued that "the best literature should deal with universals and rise above the mundane levels of social protest" (Barksdale and Kinnamon 656). Such questions suggest that protest literature, like other master narrative forms, tends to narrow the field of human experience and limit artistic possibilities. According to Baldwin: "The failure of the protest novel lies in its rejection of life, the human being, the denial of his beauty, dread, power, in its insistence that it is his [race] categorization alone which is real and which cannot be transcended" (Baldwin, *Notes* 17). Baldwin's openly gay identity often put him into conflict with the Civil Rights leadership of the 1950s (NAACP and SCLC) and the young militant leaders of the late 1960s black protest movement (Larry Neal, Eldridge Cleaver). Baldwin's "outsider" status as a homosexual was perhaps one of the motivations for his insistence on pushing the thematic limitations imposed by the protest novel form as defined by novels such as Richard Wright's *Native Son*. Despite his criticism of the protest novel form, however, Baldwin's novels and plays (like *Blues for Mister*

Charlie) embrace and advance the struggle against race oppression in the United States. Baldwin simply expected more of literature than a binary, oppositional portrayal of human experience.

Like Baldwin, Zoë Wicomb is critical of the prescriptive form of protest literature which surfaces in the current debates among South African literary critics posed as "revolutionary vs. aesthetic or good vs. bad" ("Agenda" 15). And Wicomb is equally resistant to the suggestion that committed writing must be sacrificed to aesthetic development in a South Africa moving beyond apartheid. Her novel *You Can't Get Lost in Cape Town* acknowledges the "preoccupation with the liberation struggle" which has been the foundation of South African protest writing ("Agenda" 16). I return to Chela Sandoval's metaphor of the automobile's differential that allows the driver to disengage one gear and engage another. Such mobility recognizes tactical engagement of shifting arenas—now gender, now ethnicity, now class, now the politics of exile. This kind of strategic deployment of subjectivities is theorized in Zoë Wicomb's critical essays and given agency in the narrative of Frieda in *You Can't Get Lost in Cape Town.*

The form of Wicomb's novel resembles the fictionalized autobiography, a genre which is a part of South African protest/postprotest literature. Miriam Tlali's *Muriel at Metropolitan* and Bessie Head's *A Question of Power* utilize this form to tell highly personal stories about black life under apartheid and the alienation of exile. But Wicomb undercuts this resemblance with a series of strategies that challenge the reader's assumptions. Certainly there are compelling parallels between the narrator-writer, Frieda, and the author, Zoë Wicomb, as Carol Sicherman's essay "Zoë Wicomb's *You Can't Get Lost in Cape Town:* The Narrator's Identity" points out. Both narrator and author were born in rural Cape Province, to "Coloured," Afrikaans-speaking parents who valued the cultural capital of English and encouraged their daughter(s) to speak it. Both Frieda and Wicomb attended university in Cape Town and emigrated to England, where Frieda publishes some short stories in magazines, soon to be released "[a]s a book" (171). Similarly, Wicomb's collection of "stories" was published as a book while she was still living in England. Sicherman, however, turns to the differences in biographical facts between the author and narrator, responding to Wicomb's own stated preference for literature, that is, literature that offers its reader "the experience of discontinuity, ambiguity, violation of our expectations or irony" ("Agenda" 14). Sicherman goes on to suggest that *Cape Town* is not so much an autobiography as a broader "depiction of the formation of South African 'Colored' identity" (113).

Identity formation under an apartheid system built upon the white-nonwhite binary is certainly at the heart of this novel—Frieda and her college friend Moira are caught between "want[ing] to be white" in their teens and "want[ing] to be full-blooded Africans" as adults (*Cape Town* 156). But the development of a South African female *writer* of color is also crucial to *Cape Town*. Even in my initial reading of the text, it was the last chapter/story that prevented me from reading this collection as simply fictionalized autobiography.

The last chapter/story acts as a metanarrative on the process of writing autobiography. Ruptures in the plot do not allow the kind of historical linearity often expected of such first-person narratives. For example, the Mamma of Frieda's childhood seems to have died by chapter 3, where she is spoken of in the past tense. Yet the final chapter records Frieda's visit home following her father's death and her mother is still very much alive. This revelation then forces the reader to doubt the legitimacy of the earlier chapters as simply a writer's imagining of a young woman/writer's maturation. Frieda struggles to make her mother understand the nature of writing: "[T]hey're only stories. Made up. Everyone knows it's not real, not the truth" (172). "But you've used the real. If I can recognise places and people, so can others, and if you want to play around like that why don't you have the courage to tell the whole truth?" asks her mother. Her mother accuses Frieda of writing "from under [her] mother's skirts" (172). This discussion of the use of personal family history, by the "real" narrator in her made-up "stories," and the invention of her mother's death, "unnecessary" because she has killed her mother "over and over" with the publication of stories about such topics as abortion, insinuates into this fictional narrative the space to speculate on the narrator's identity as well as the boundaries between autobiography and fiction. Using this last chapter as a lens, subsequent readings reveal that Wicomb provides hints throughout that what we are reading are Frieda's "stories," not Frieda's or Wicomb's autobiography.

Early in the novel, Wicomb plants in the reader's mind a distrust of the reliability of writing. While at the university at Cape Town, Frieda struggles to write an essay on Thomas Hardy's *Tess of the D'Urbervilles* but is unable to express what she really feels. She imagines the confrontation with her Boer professor had she gone to his office asking for an extension; she studies the pen in her hand; she rereads her lecture notes: "The novel, he says, is about Fate. Alarmingly simple, but not quite how it strikes me, although I cannot offer an alternative. . . . Seduced, my notes say. Can you be seduced by someone you hate?" (41). Frieda longs to produce an essay that resists the professor's interpretation but opts instead for a "reworking of his notes" which will assure her a "mark qualifying for the examination" (55). Tess is "branded guilty and betrayed once more on this page," sacrificed to Frieda's pragmatic desire for academic success (56). Frieda's "betrayal" of Tess hinges on doing what is expedient rather than submitting a genuine expression of her opinion, warning the reader that we cannot always trust the written word or the professional expert.

Evidence that Frieda believes oral first-person narratives are also unreliable comes in a visit home prior to leaving for England; Frieda describes the way her family tell stories about themselves:

> They cut their stories from the gigantic watermelon that cannot be finished by the family in one sitting. They savour as if for the first time the pip-studded slices of the bright fruit and read the possibilities of konfyt in the tasteless flesh beneath the green. Their stories, whole as the watermelon that grows out of this arid earth, have come to replace the world. (87)

She wants to expose the fallacy of wholeness shaped by these family stories:

> I would like to bring down my fist on that wholeness and watch the crack choose its wayward path across the melon, slowly exposing the icy pink of the slit. I would like to reveal myself now so that they will not await my return. But they will not like my stories, none of them. (87–88)

The family stories deny aspects of Frieda's experience and her intent to leave South Africa and never return. Frieda's desire to smash this monochromatic representation of collective experience reveals a striving toward recognition of individual difference. But reading Frieda's desire for "truth" through the revelations in the final chapter of *Cape Town* reveals that Frieda's autobiography is as consciously constructed as is the family folklore: neither is to be trusted at face value.

Wicomb also blurs the boundaries of fiction and biography in the chapter/story titled "A Fair Exchange." This chapter begins like a fictional short story; through a male narrator's descriptions and through dialogue between characters, we read about rural life on the veld—his struggle to survive and the loss of his wife and children to another man. This tale of South African sheepherder Skitterboud seems to mark a jarring departure from the previous chapters which hitherto have shaped Frieda's autobiography. Near the end of the chapter, we discover that this is really one of Frieda's "stories," collected from Skitterboud on a trip home. The reader is warned that Skitterboud's first-person narrative is edited and revised in her reconstruction of it:

> Skitterboud's story is yellow with age. It curls without question at the edges. Many years have passed since the events settled into a picture which then was torn in sadness and rage so that now reassembled the cracks remain too clear. . . . A few fragments are irretrievably lost. Or are they? If I pressed even further . . . I am responsible for reassembling the bits released over the days that I sought him out. (136)

Ownership of Skitterboud's story changes hands with the exchange of a pair of spectacles. Frieda is wearing at first them, but they also improve Skitterboud's vision when he tries them on. Frieda takes the spectacles back, insisting that he must have his own glasses/vision "specially prescribed" for him. But her lens(es) allows Skitterboud to "see" better and he insists that she leave the spectacles with him: "Who can know better than myself whether these glasses are good for me or not?" (139–40). The spectacles represent a narrative strategy that reconfigures Skitterboud's life. Frieda's narrative re-visioning of Skitterboud's story allows him to see the present better and to reconcile certain aspects of his past. The "whole truth" that Mamma wants Frieda to have the courage to tell consists in the negotiation between the subject and his biographer, the autobiographical writer and her reader.

Wicomb invokes distrust of discursive representation and provides a metanarrative discussion about writing in the final chapter of *You Can't Get Lost in Cape Town,* blurring the distinction between art and life: is this Frieda's story or is it her art (fiction)? The idea that the previous "chapters" can be read as Frieda's stories is not apparent until the final chapter, and this arrangement necessitates a second reading of the text. An actively engaged reading practice demands that, as readers, we allow ourselves to be drawn into the narrative and that we respond to the demands made on us by the text, that we be willing to negotiate with it. Wicomb's narrative arrangement in *Cape Town* is representative of the kind of postmodernist strategy developed by her South African literary constituency (Tlali, Head, Gordimer, Coetzee). But in the case of colonized artists, the tendency to push beyond established boundaries is also accompanied by the dialectics inherent in colonialism and the literature of protest which is its direct oppositional response.

Binary constructions limit our perceptions of the human experience in literature; an unsympathetic read of the binary relationships extant in postprotest literature of colonized people denies the context, the material context and objective reality, in which such literature is produced. Wicomb troubles the distinction between art and life, but a politically committed reader will not fail to situate her textual manipulations in the literary context against which such manipulations work. The intersecting sites of gender, race/ethnicity, and economic class provide Wicomb with a wedge with which to pry open the black versus white binary inherent in the discourses of the apartheid state and the anti-apartheid forces as portrayed in protest literature. Student protest in Lewis Nkosi's play *The Rhythm of Violence,* for instance, portrays activists of several racial groups, but the structure of its scenes suggests a typical two-sided struggle with a unified body of student anti-apartheid activists, on the one side, against the white administration, on the other. Similarly, in her chapter/story "A Clearing in the Bush," Wicomb gives us an example of student protest at the "Coloured" university which her character Frieda attends. However, in order to show the ruptures within coalition politics, Wicomb's portrait moves beyond a depiction of a diverse but unified student body dedicated to a single cause.

In Wicomb's novel, the image of the student protest movement, as a kind of monolith, is challenged by gender politics. When the university is closed for a memorial service for the infamous and recently assassinated Prime Minister Verwoerd, the male students meet in the cafeteria to plan a boycott of the service and to determine the method by which all students should be notified of this political action. Frieda and her friend Moira observe the meeting and ask their friend James what it is about. Although James has been sent to enlist their support, he "nurse[s] the apple of knowledge in his lap," making the most of their anticipation, offering them "little lady-like bites," aware of "his power to withdraw it altogether" (53). The student action is planned and controlled by the men, and the cooperation of the women is assumed. James constructs the narrative; Frieda and Moira must be passive recipients. Such chasms between men and women are often concealed in the discursive representation of protest movements for the sake of unity. But Wicomb is clear that sexism need not be tolerated for the sake of black solidarity. In her contribution to a forum on feminism and writing in South Africa, sponsored by and published in *Current Writing: Text and Reception in Southern Africa* in 1990, Wicomb states: "I can think of no reason why black patriarchy should not be challenged alongside the fight against Apartheid" ("To Hear" 37). Wicomb's narrative portrayal of gender politics within the student protest movement reflects the disjunctures in hegemonic discourses, revealing one concern of postmodernity and post-coloniality in Third World texts and environments. Wicomb further complicates her portrait of the student body by challenging the assumed cohesion of colored identity and the anti-apartheid movement.

Despite the need for total support of the boycott in order to avoid reprisals for a few, some students attend the memorial. Several "Coloured" young men from the seminary, "future Dutch Reformed ministers," file in, dressed "in their Sunday suits. . . . They walk in silence, their chins lifted in a militaristic display of courage. . . . [T]hey . . . think their defiance heroic and stifle the unease by marching soldier-like to mourn the Prime Minister" (56). The action taken by the seminary students is a trope that seeks to provoke in the reader a distrust of nationalist propaganda that is always trying to cover up the cracks of dissension. Such disjunctures in postprotest narratives do not, however, diminish real oppositional relationships created by colonial and race oppression, but simply illuminate different subjectivities and the forces that determine them. In her essay "Postcoloniality and Postmodernity," Wicomb demonstrates how ethnicity and linguistics determine shifting alliances across the spectrum of difference and disjuncture in the would-be unitary discourse of the anti-apartheid movement. The idea that the seminary students believe their action "heroic" indicates their co-optation by the very system that has allowed the white minority population to so successfully and brutally maintain control of the majority. Wicomb's essay points out that in the Cape, the "Coloured" population makes up a significant majority (52% compared with 25% African and 23% white). The Nationalist Party's about-face from a policy of racial separation to an appeal to this bloc of new voters on the basis of "shared culture centred in the Afrikaans language, the Dutch Reformed church and mutton bredie" and the majority Cape Coloured vote in favor of the Nationalist Party constitute, in Wicomb's words, a "postmodern effacement of history stretch[ing] back to the very practice of slavery" (9). Wicomb's discussion here calls attention to the way in which the pro-black and pro-English language position of the anti-apartheid movement, which is tantamount to a form of nationalism, erases and alienates some South Africans identified as "Coloured," particularly those whose mother tongue, Afrikaans, and whose religious customs originate in the Dutch Reformed Church.

While these seminary students represent a dissenting fracture within the student population, Wicomb also calls attention to the effacement of working-class "Coloured" from the student boycott. The narrative voice in this chapter switches back and forth between Frieda and an omniscient narrator who reveals the interior life of Tamieta, the lone female "Coloured" cook in the university's cafeteria. Her boss notifies her of the memorial ceremony, and Tamieta assumes that he means for her to attend the activity, only to discover that she is the only person there besides the Boers. She begins to fear that the memorial is for whites only, but she is somewhat comforted when the seminary students enter. When no other students arrive, Tamieta begins to understand that a boycott has been called. She thinks to herself, in a typical working-class female fashion: "If only there were other women working on the campus she would have known, someone would have told her" (60). Of course there are other women/people on campus, but they are the students who did not think to alert the cook whose labor sustains them daily. As the young "future Dutch Reformed ministers" call attention to the complexity of racial politics in South Africa, Tamieta reveals class as a blind spot in some versions of coalition. While Wicomb complicates Nkosi's version of the student struggle in South Africa with diverse subject positions, her inclusion of this movement in a chapter/story about Frieda's university experience signals its continuing import in South African fiction.

Likewise, the loss of South African land to Boer "land reform," with the resulting reservationlike townships and "native reserves," are insistent issues in protest and postprotest fiction alike. A reader who chooses active engagement as a reading practice might find Tlali's treatment of forced relocation and its effects on black South African women, for instance, a rich source for intertextual connections with Wicomb's *Cape Town*. Reading Wicomb's postprotest text against Tlali's depiction of black South African displacement raises questions about the intersections of economic class and racial classification under apartheid. Wicomb revisits the Group Areas Act in her portrait of the narrator's uncle, Jan Klinkies, who has lost his sanity and his wife along with his land. But Wicomb's narrator seems untroubled by her father's announcement that they must leave the veld for the village of Wesblok. The child's-eye view Frieda re-creates of her family's loss of ancestral home reveals the attenuating effect of middle-class status on personal suffering caused by displacement. Frieda's father is a rural schoolmaster who has a "nest egg" that will pay her tuition at the newly desegregated private school. Unlike Tlali's characters who live in labor camps and multifamily township houses, Frieda's father will buy a "little raw brick house [with] somewhere to tether a goat and keep a few chickens" (*Cape Town* 29). Young Frieda thinks that electric lights, indoor plumbing, and the proximity to friends provided by community housing might not be so bad. While many of Tlali's black female characters find limited options in urban life and must rely on the remnants of traditional support systems, Frieda leaves the village for university in Cape Town and then moves to England, where she becomes a writer. Class position, determined in part by apartheid's racial structure, allows Frieda opportunities to which Tlali's female characters do not have access. But at the same time, Wicomb's juxtaposition of Frieda with Tamieta, the cook at the university Frieda attends, disrupts the assumption that socioeconomic class marks the "Coloured" population of South Africa in any monolithic way.

Wicomb's novel also enacts the ethnic diversity obscured by apartheid's "Coloured" classification, the liberation movement's unifying embrace of "black," and the postapartheid adoption of "Coloured" by the reactionary forces at the Cape. Frieda grows up in a "Coloured" community, but ethnic bias marks this community. In *Cape Town,* it is Frieda's father who most often bears the burden of demonstrating it. When Frieda is a child, her father invokes ethnic difference in order to urge her to eat: "'Don't leave anything on your plate. You must grow up to be big and strong. . . . You don't want cheekbones that jut out like a Hottentot's. Fill them out until they're shiny and plump as pumpkins" (24). And when Frieda returns to South Africa after several years spent in England, he tells her that the formerly segregated doctor's office has changed: "[T]here's even a waiting room for us now with a nice clean water lavatory. Not that these Hotnos know how to use it" (105). The colonialist term for the indigenous South African population, "Hottentot," becomes an epithet of ethnic prejudice. Most of Frieda's family are Namaqua, one of the subdivisions of the Khoi, the original Cape inhabitants, but her father values his "Scots blood" and his Shenton surname (29). When he first met Frieda's mother, she was disparaged by the Shentons as a "Griqua meid" (165), and she in turn uses the term "Griqua" to chastise a young Frieda who is misbehaving (9).

In addition to disrupting the homogeneity of "Coloured" identity with class and ethnicity, Wicomb's novel raises the issue of colonially imposed language. As a child, Frieda is forbidden to speak Afrikaans; both parents value English and model their pronunciation after an English mine owner who frequents the village. English language becomes cultural capital at Frieda's private high school and the university in Cape Town. I first read Wicomb's portrayal of the Shentons' veneration of English through what I knew at that time of the liberation movement's resistance, expressed during the 1976 Soweto uprising, to the imposition of Afrikaans language as the medium of instruction in South African schools. English language represented not only cultural capital but also an expression of solidarity with black resistance. But Wicomb's essay "Postcoloniality and Postmodernity: The Case of the Coloured in South Africa" complicates that assumption. Wicomb points out that Afrikaans was the first language of the "Cape coloureds," who originated as a product of sexual union between the Dutch settlers and indigenous inhabitants. Their response to the resistance movement's English language mandate was to embrace a nonstandard form of Afrikaans in a "flurry of coloured writing. . . . Renamed and revalorized as Kaaps, this local and racialised variety of Afrikaans as a literary language came to assert a discursive space for an oppositional colouredness that could be aligned to the black liberation struggle" (7). My assumption that textual cues signaled Wicomb's black solidarity obscured the complexity of the language issue among the "Coloured" community of South Africa. A reader who claims empathy with his or her reading subject, who is practicing a transnational feminist approach to reading, should be willing to engage in renegotiations with the text in light of such revelations.

The South African experience when organized as a narrative of protest "reflects a sort of weave of presence and absence," to borrow a phrase from Gayatri Spivak in her essay "The Problem of Cultural Self-Representation" (50). What is always present is the hegemonic binary of race, black versus white, or the binary of colonizer versus the colonized. But Wicomb's text restores many of the erasures imposed by colonial representations and strategically adopted by anticolonial resistance. With the anticipation of the demise of the apartheid structure, postprotest texts, like *You Can't Get Lost in Cape Town,* are opening up prescriptive forms of protest writing and binary representations. While some writers such as Coetzee and Gordimer imagine apocalyptic endings to apartheid, Wicomb's postprotest text is set in a society still very much structured by it. Frieda has tried to escape to England, but Wicomb's text does not seem to support exile as a solution. Frieda's years in England constitute an erasure in the narrative. Frieda never writes any "stories" about it; her memories of life there conflate the uncomfortably cold winter and her sense of racial otherness. Like Bessie Head's Margaret (*Maru*) and Eliz-abeth (*A Question of Power*), whose ethnic difference isolates them from the larger communities in which they live, Frieda's period of expatriation is one of alienation. But unlike Head's texts, *Cape Town* leaves this pe-riod unexplored. Frieda returns to Cape Town and achieves a modified reconciliation with her mother, while insisting on her prerogative to write stories.

What Wicomb's postapartheid essays make clear is that, in her view, the end of apartheid has not yet been achieved. No revolution marks its passing. An essay in which Wicomb reflects about having been asked to judge an interracial literary competition expresses her concern for the brutal inequities which are the legacy of apartheid:

> In our situation, where apartheid conditions have militated against the linguistic development of black people, both in the imposition of Euro-pean languages and the neglect of education, the function of the liter-ary prize becomes obvious. Not only is it inappropriate or inadequate as a means of encouraging writing, but it actively perpetuates inequity by rewarding those who have been privileged. ("Culture Beyond Color?" 28)

At the root of this issue is literacy. Wicomb calls for a "decent, compul-sory, multilingual system of education for all" before any interracial con-struction of a new South Africa can be valid (32).

Wicomb suggests that instead of erasing a social history which reveals diversity and constructing nationalistic unities, South African "Coloured" identity could be staged as "multiple belongings" ("Post-coloniality" 14). It is through Wicomb's representation of the tenuous-ness of "Coloured" identity that I have approached an analysis of her text. And it is this idea of "multiple belongings" that might serve as a metaphor for transnational feminist reading. An empathic desire to lo-cate the fissures in hegemonic representations of "others" is one way to resist the generative power of colonial domination and capitalist ex-ploitation. A reading practice that desires to find points of commonality across difference might want to examine, in the writing of South African female authors such as Wicomb, the discursive strategies which resist "hierarchising the evils of . . . society—racism, sexism, classism" and instead attend to the "ways in which the conflicting demands of repre-senting these are textually articulated" ("To Hear" 42).

NOTES

[1]This essay was originally written as a conference paper and presented in abbreviated form as a plenary address at the African Language Association (ALA) conference in March 1995 (Columbus). Quotations here are from the original essay, kindly provided by the author.

[2]Also known as the Nationalist Party of South Africa.

[3]Wicomb lays claim to a black political identity in her essay "An Author's Agenda," published in 1990, prior to majority rule in South Africa; she reiterated this position at the 1995 ALA conference.

[4]From Miriam Tlali, *Muriel at Metropolitan* (Essex: Longman, 1987) 169.

[5]These indigenous people were referred to as "Hottentot," an infamous term in colonialist constructions of southern Africa.

[6]These are urban street gangs of young people. The implication is that their intimidation tactics are not simply ignored by the justice system but that their guns and knives may be provided by corrupt police.

[7]It is possible that the footnotes in particular are a result of choices on the part of the publisher rather than the author. The edition I am working from, *Soweto Stories,* was published by Pandora Press in London and perhaps targeted toward an international audience. This collection was also published in South Africa by David Phillip Publisher Ltd. under the title *Footprints in the Quag: Stories and Dialogues from Soweto.* Either way, the effect is the same. As a non–South African reader, I am left feeling that there is less investigation and negotiation required of me than when reading a postprotest/postmodernist work like Wicomb's *Cape Town.*

CHAPTER 4

Exoticism to Transnational Feminism: Alice Walker

> *[W]as it the drumbeats, messengers of the*
> *sacred dance of life and deathlessness on earth?*
> *Must I still long to be within the black circle*
> *around the red, glowing fire, to feel the breath*
> *of love hot against my cheeks, the smell of love*
> *strong about my waiting thighs! Must I still*
> *tremble at the thought of the passions stifled*
> *beneath this voluminous rustling snow!*
>
> (WALKER, "Diary" 115)

> *[T]o find out any part of the truth, women must*
> *travel themselves where they hope to find it. In*
> *my opinion and experience, imperialists of all*
> *nations and races will tell us anything to keep*
> *us fighting. For them.*
>
> (WALKER, "To the Editors" 352)

Of particular importance in discussing the internal fragmentation of African peoples are the diasporic and indigenous responses to enslavement and colonization of the pre- and postindependence eras. The "invention" of Africa in the political and literary imaginings of African peoples, continental and diasporic, represents a contested space divided along the lines of culture and nationality upon which location, positionality, and identity construction determine political practices that extend to the acts of writing and reading texts. The selected works of Alice Walker, which are the concern of this chapter, are representative of a transnational writing practice that reflects the strategic deployment of subjectivities across national and cultural boundaries, articulating a kind of identity politics that complicates binary constructions of race and colonialism with the intervention of her international feminist perspective. In considering Walker's approach to the predicament of women in colonial and patriarchal societies, one must recognize that there are no sacred places; Walker's critique of patriarchal practices against the bodies of women transcends the politics of white versus black, colonizer versus colonized, and addresses forms of cultural nationalism that appropriate traditional African patriarchal practices as anticolonial strategies. Alice Walker's *The Color Purple* (1982), *The Temple of My Familiar* (1989), *Possessing the Secret of Joy* (1992), and the coauthored *Warrior Marks* (1993) claim race and gender as international identities and criticize the violence perpetrated upon these aspects of identity and played out on the bodies of women by both patriarchal colonizers and patriarchal indigenous governments.

In her creation of female voices, Walker conveys a variety of shared experiences representative of diasporic African women in the United States and continental women of Africa, and in so doing imagines a kind of Pan-African female selfhood. This concept of identity has been criticized by some African women because of the stand Walker has taken against female genital mutilation; they claim that her location as a Western humanist and diasporic African locates her experience outside the realities of continental African women. This critique should be examined as it seems to question the appropriateness of an international configuration of race and gender, stirs the problematic debate around authenticity of voice, and underscores women's internal fragmentation under patriarchy. Yet, at the same time, in their introduction to *Scattered Hegemonies,* Inderpal Grewal and Caren Kaplan charge women who are committed to transnational feminist practice not to allow a "cultural defense" argument to deter the effort to uncover cultural and institutional links among transnational power structures that oppress women. Walker's approach, in these later texts, resists the cultural defense accusation and constitutes a transnational feminist practice. This chapter will approach Walker's later work by tracing Walker's transnational, anti-imperialist consciousness as it develops alongside her critique of patriarchy. Examples of Walker's earlier essays and fiction demonstrate a strategy of thinking and rethinking, recounting personal events and experiences shared with other women evidencing "an incorrigible sense of one-worldism," a world although fragmented by difference, "joined" by common experience and shared enmity of imperialist domination ("To the Editors" 352). This earlier work can inform how we interpret her later novels. For the purposes of this discussion, it is precisely Walker's critical imagining of African female selfhood under the conditions of traditional patriarchy and colonialism that qualifies her as a practitioner of a postcolonial transnational feminist writing practice.

Walker enters the arena of controversy not merely on the grounds of her critique of female initiation rites among continental African cultures but also on the broader issue of her criticism of patriarchal practices against the humanity of women everywhere. Walker has received criticism from African American critics (e.g., Trudier Harris, Cheatwood) for the representation of black men in her novels. However, what these criticisms do not take notice of is that, for Walker, as for her literary foremother Zora Neale Hurston, to disregard the existence of male oppression of women would be a turning away from the realities that women have historically faced.

Walker's approach to the construction of her female characters is further complicated not only by her international and transnational consciousness, and by her tenacious insistence upon revealing the links between gender oppression and race oppression, but also by her class location as a petit bourgeois intellectual. Her class location seems to have determined the course of self-fulfillment and self-actualization of her female characters, many of whom are representative subjects of the American success story and master narrative strategies, leading some Marxist critics to lament such valorization of bourgeois materialism.

The following discussion will, therefore, examine how Walker utilizes the displacement that is the heritage of the "black Atlantic" experience, specifically her location as an African American subject of domestic neocolonialism in the United States, to create a colonial subtext in her work which facilitates the articulation of a transnational feminist writing practice. Since Walker is a diasporic African writer who writes across cultural boundaries, I am particularly interested in her imaginings and stylized treatment of the effects of colonization in Africa, her demonstration of the effects of colonial subjugation and indigenous patriarchy on indigenous women of Africa, and how these strategies constitute a transnational writing practice.

AFRICA AND WALKER'S LITERARY IMAGINATION

Through her characters, Alice Walker, like Virginia Woolf and Zoë Wicomb, represents the colonial process as it affects the female body. Her own heritage of displacement locates Walker as an "outsider" within the United States, a neocolonial economic power in the late twentieth century. She operates as an "insider" in relation to her African sisters on the basis of shared race, sex, and ancestry, but as an "outsider" lacking shared cultural experience when she chooses to explore the imposition of traditional practices on continental African women's bodies as a site of struggle and when she deploys her diasporic imagination in the construction of African women's experiences. It is in *Possessing the Secret of Joy* and the subsequent *Warrior Marks* that Walker most clearly claims insider status and for which she is most soundly criticized as an "outsider." However, her stance in these later works should come as no surprise, but rather can be seen as the logical outcome of a developing Pan-African literary imagination. One of her earliest associations with African female selfhood is rendered in an important short story through the character of an African nun and subsequently the critique of Christian missionization in Africa.

As early as 1968, when "Diary of an African Nun" was published in *Freedomways,* Walker was using her fiction to draw attention to the way Western religion must be seen as complicit in cultural colonization and in the oppression of women. Her unnamed first-person narrator has grown up in a Ugandan village at the foot of the Ruwenzori mountains, was educated in the mission school, and is now "a wife of Christ, a wife of the Catholic church" (114). She lives among the priests and nuns, whose lives seemed "regal" and "productive" to her as a child but which she now characterizes as cold, barren, and "[s]hrouded in whiteness" (114). We come to know the narrator through her six diary entries in which she laments her loss of the possibity of marriage and children, granted to the others of her village, and reveals her dismay over the physical passion which the nightly drumbeats from the village stir in her. Walker's African nun likens her "marriage" to a "bodiless" lover (the Catholic Church) to the "hot black soil" of the mountains, "stifled" beneath "voluminous, rustling snow" (115). Her indigenous cultural practices become a sensual "dance of life," the spring which brings birth and rebirth. She regrets the part she must play in silencing the drumbeats and stifling this dance by turning the villagers' eyes to an "empty sky" (118).

The sterility of her life as a Catholic nun is assailed by erotic imaginings which signify the commodified tropes (cliché, pastiche) of romance narratives as evidenced by the first epigraph for this chapter. Walker's exotic and erotic phraseology, however, does not exploit African selfhood to create a European one as in some master narratives, but rather functions to lament the captivity of the villagers' (pro)creative forces, "the dance of life and the urgent fire of creation" by the imposition of Western religious doctrine. The colonial project inscribed in Walker's narrative is expressed in metaphors: the white habit that covers her character's body, and the snow, an "icy whiteness" that "shrouds" the mountain peaks above the village. In one entry the nun resists the devaluation of indigenous spirituality; she imagines addressing her "husband":

> Dearly Beloved, let me tell you about the mountains and the spring. The mountains that we see around us are black, it is the snow that gives them their icy whiteness. In the spring, the hot black soil melts the crust of the snow on the mountains, and the water as it runs down the sheets of fiery rock burns and cleanses the naked bodies that come to wash in it. It is when the snows melt that the people here plant their crops; the soil of the mountains is rich, and its produce plentiful and good. . . . [W]hat is my faith in the spring and the eternal melting of snows (you will ask) but your belief in the Resurrection? Could I convince one so wise that my belief bears more fruit? (117–18)

As the "hot black soil" has the power to melt its icy blanket in the spring, the indigenous peoples of her village, of her country, of Africa, have the potential to dismantle the shroud of colonial domination. The "melting snows" can "cleanse" the people; the enriched soil can bear "more fruit."

However, while Walker's nun may recognize the power of the oppressed to throw off the oppressor, she seems resigned, by her last diary entry, to the insidious nature of missionary Christianity as a tool of colonial control, and struggles with her own collusion in containing "the dance of life":

> My mouth must be silent, then, though my heart jumps to the booming of the drums, as to the last strong pulse of life in a dying world.
>
> For the drums will soon, one day, be silent. I will help muffle them forever. To assure life for my people in this world I must be among the lying ones and teach them how to die. . . .

> In this way will the wife of a loveless, barren, hopeless Western marriage broadcast the joys of an enlightened religion to an imitative people. (118)

The nun's acknowledgment of her complicity in a project that, though perhaps well intentioned, displaces the indigenous people from their land and alienates the "converted" from a long-standing way of life will appear again in Nettie's last letters to Celie (*The Color Purple*), where she expresses some of the same concerns. Walker's creation of self-critical female narrators, a converted continental African and a missionizing (diasporic) African American, respectively, represents an attempt to complicate the binary politics of race and colonialism suggesting the fragmentation of national-individual consciousness articulated by such philosophers as W. E. B. Du Bois, Frantz Fanon, and Homi Bhabha. These narrators represent Walker's early explorations of the connections between African and African American women on the basis of a shared gender and displacement by hegemonic systems (patriarchy/Christianity). It is not merely the patriarchal family with which Walker's works are concerned, but also the suppression of women by a masculine god concept. Hence, the diary entry addressed by Walker's African nun to her god-husband signifies her recognition of the collusion between patriarchy and Western religion. The self-reflexive, self-critical consciousness that Walker demonstrates in Nettie and her unnamed nun not only suggests the alienation of these Westernized individuals but might also point to Walker's own self-reflexivity as a privileged diasporic African in an industrially advanced, predominately white and Christian society, and how this position and location fits within the matrix of social contradictions, conflicts, and resolutions on the international scale.

The significance of Walker's narrators who question their own complicity in the project of colonial domination and her developing transnational consciousness is further illuminated by some of her nonfiction writing. Perhaps the most compelling example is her 1977 essay "My Father's Country Is the Poor," published in *In Search of Our Mothers' Gardens*. Walker writes about her mid-1970s visit to Cuba. She and other African American cultural workers, selected by the editors of the *Black Scholar,* spent two weeks as guests of the Cuban Institute for Friendship Among Peoples in communion with Cuban artists. Walker recollects her meeting with Pablo Díaz, who, before the Cuban Revolution, "might have belonged to any country, or to none, so poor was he" (214). In drawing attention to the physical resemblance between Díaz and her own father, a sharecropper from rural Georgia, Walker sets up a comparison of their class positions and realizes how the socialist revolution has transformed the class structure of Cuba and afforded Díaz an opportunity that her own father never had. Like her father, Díaz had been a peasant:

> So unlikely it would have been for anyone in the government to wonder or care what he wanted of life, what he thought, what he observed. He had cut cane, done the "Hey *boy!*" jobs of the big cities (Havana and New York), and had joined the revolution early—an option my father never had. From the anonymity he shared with my father, Pablo Díaz had fought his way to the other side of existence; and it is from his lips that many visitors to Cuba learn the history of the Cuban struggle. (214)

The encounter reminds Walker of an earlier revelation, when, at the age of seventeen, she left home for college. Walker realized that the newly acquired middle-class status afforded her by virtue of her being a college student, from that moment forward, would be a barrier between herself and her father, a "brilliant man—great at mathematics, unbeatable at storytelling, but unschooled beyond the primary grades" (216). A writer's awareness of language, in this instance, can be a dangerous and painful enlightenment. Walker laments in this essay that the language she acquired at college did not foster closeness with her father nor facilitate communication with him; rather it "obscured more than it revealed" (216). Her matriculation into bourgeois status laid bare the duality of her selfhood as an expatriated, one-generation-removed daughter of a sharecropping family. As she left her father "by the side of that lonely Georgia highway," the tears in her eyes were of "guilt *and* relief" (216, emphasis added). It is this rift between father and daughter that "poverty engenders. It is what injustice means" (216). Unlike for Pablo Díaz, there was no metamorphosis possible for Walker's father or for their relationship.

In Cuba, however, Walker is able to imagine the possibilities created by social revolution. She is keenly aware of how armed struggle against class oppression and the (re)construction of society, guided by a socialist vision, has the potential to erode age-based, race-based, and gender-based antagonism. Pablo Díaz's transformation from "peasant to official historian" serves as Walker's example of how genuine access to education encourages the elder societal members "to grow, to develop, to change, to 'keep up with' their children. To become *compañeros* as well as parents" (215). The wedge that her education forced between Walker and her father need not be a barrier between the children and parents of postrevolution Cuba.

Efforts to eliminate the race-based antagonism in this country of African and Spanish heritage, whose "'dominant culture' is recognized as being a synthesis of the two," were of particular interest to Walker and her party of African American artists and writers (210). Responding to their dismay at the presence of waiters who were exclusively black, the Cuban hosts admitted that before the revolution, domestic service was performed disproportionately by blacks but that what has changed is that now no group is permanently relegated to servitude of any kind but everyone has access to free education, with the opportunity to prepare and test for other positions. Upon visiting day-care centers and public schools, the group saw further proof of Cuba's commitment to dismantle the institutional structures that reinforce race-based privilege. No distinctions are made on the basis of race or gender; all students wear uniforms and study all academic disciplines. It was observing the younger generation's lack of race consciousness that forced Walker to interrogate her own Western, bourgeois assumptions about race and to accept responsibility for her need to forge a cross-cultural identity politics on the basis of race. Walker notes that, in response to the visitors distinguishing themselves as *black* Americans, the children seemed, for the first time, "aware of color differences *among themselves—and were embarrassed for us*" (212). At this point, Walker admits that she had been unconsciously categorizing the children on the basis of race while the children's sense of group identity was based, instead, on a sense of nation that is Cuban and socialist. It was/is black Americans, living in a state where race and class too often intertwine and ensnare people of color in a web of oppression, who have a vested interest in maintaining a consciousness of race.

Just as the elimination of institutional racism has been a goal of the revolutionary government of Cuba, so has gender-based oppression. Walker recounts seeing female workers in many areas—"doctors, laborers, heads of publishing companies, and so on, as well as teachers, nurses, and directors of child-care centers" (217). Equal access to free education must be matched with genuinely open hiring policies in industry. But further, the Cuban Family Code targets prerevolutionary gender-role assumptions in the family, demanding that both partners share the responsibility for the operation and support of the home and for the care of children. And while Walker notes that, at the time of her visit, she encountered few female writers or filmmakers, she suggests that this will follow as a logical result of state-mandated equal access. Disturbing to Walker, however, are personal attitudes that seem to glorify a European beauty aesthetic for women, an aesthetic which can be achieved by many Cuban women only by radically altering their natural appearance. Walker suggests that the fetishization of European female beauty might indicate that gender- and race-based antagonism has not yet been completely eliminated.

While Walker is troubled by this beauty aesthetic, by the dearth of women as writers and filmmakers, and by the race consciousness of some of the older members of Cuban society (which she sees in the older white members of the Union of Cuban Writers and the Institute of Cuban Films), she concedes that, as Fidel Castro teaches, "revolution is not a flash in the pan of injustice. It is . . . 'a process,' " and that with the support of social institutions, such personal attitudes will likely change with the next generation (209).

What Walker finds most disturbing on her Cuban trip are the state-supported sanctions against homosexuality. The revolutionary government's emphasis on rebuilding the (heterosexual) Cuban family denies the possibility of gay family life and mandates that homosexuals may not teach, become doctors, or hold any positions that might influence children. While Walker and her party wholly embrace Cuba's efforts to eradicate age-, race-, gender-, and class-based oppression, she realizes that her gay and lesbian friends would not have felt the immediate sense of racial community that she felt as a heterosexual in Cuba; the strictures placed on gay life by the revolutionary government are unacceptable to Walker. She concludes her essay by expressing hope that the Cuban people who have worked so hard to "alleviate the burdens of the dispossessed . . . will become ever more sensitive to those who are now dispossessed by the revolution" (221).

It is in interrogating the response of other "First World" visitors to postrevolutionary Cuba that Walker suggests the potential of a transnational perspective. In the Cuba that existed prior to the Soviet collapse, Walker sees for herself what a socialist revolution has meant to the people of Cuba:

> Many Americans who visit Cuba complain that life there is hard. And it is. But they do not seem adequately impressed by the fact that poverty has been eliminated, or that nearly all the people can read. . . . They do not say—as I feel—that a hard life shared equally by all is preferable to a life of ease and plenty enjoyed by a few. Standing in line

for hours to receive one's daily bread cannot be so outrageous if it means every person *will receive bread,* and no one will go to bed hungry at night. (203)

Walker's experience of "world travelling" in the absence of "arrogant perception" (Lugones 1990) leads her to recommend that "to find out any part of the truth, women must travel *themselves* where they hope to find it. . . . [I]mperialists of all nations and races will tell us anything to keep us fighting. For them" ("To the Editors" 352).

Such world traveling does not preclude historical reality. Walker comes to recognize that, although joined in common oppression, oppressed peoples are still fragmented by their specific histories. For example, African Americans, who in the past were the uncritical allies of Jews based upon a shared sense of persecution, continue to show as much sympathy and outright solidarity with Palestinians in the 1980s and 1990s. In her essay "To the Editors of *Ms.* Magazine," Walker recalls a Jewish friend, considered by her (Walker's) Jewish ex-husband to be a traitor to Israel because of her expressed solidarity with the Palestinian women she had visited in refugee camps in the 1960s. Although sympathetic to her husband's heritage of persecution and to aspirations of the Jewish people to maintain a homeland, Walker is divided, recognizing the Palestinian right to nation as well. It is her Jewish friend who notices not only how much the Jewish and Palestinian women share, but also that across national identities and despite competition for land, the Palestinian women desired the support of this Jewish woman:

She did not assume Palestinian women "wished her dead," and she was happily surprised to discover they did not. She did discover she looked a lot like them (dark and Semitic: 'Cousins my ass,' she said, '*sisters,* or somebody's mirror is lying'), that they shared many historical and cultural similarities, and that Palestinian women were no more wedded to the notion of violence than she was. (352)

While Walker is deeply moved by her friend's courage and her emotional support for her Palestinian sisters, she cannot help but acknowledge the fault lines, big and small, between women of different nationalities. Walker remains critical of the kind of Jewish feminism that in the final analysis advocates Zionism. But she is equally critical of anti-Semitism that fails to recognize that homeless people also have a right to a "place." She is cautious of the tendency of some African Americans to embrace ideologies of reaction as antidotes to other reactionary ideologies. In her response to a 1982 article by Letty Cottin Pogrebin titled "Anti-Semitism in the Women's Movement," Walker urges:

> Jewish feminists will have to try to understand people of color's hatred of imperialism and colonialism: we who have lost whole continents to the white man's arrogance and greed, and to his white female accomplice's inability to say no to stolen gold, diamonds, and furs. And yes, I suspect Jewish feminists *will* have to identify as Jews within feminism with as much discomfort as they identify as feminists within Judaism; every other woman of an oppressed group has always experienced this double bind. And people of color will have to try to understand Jewish fears of another Holocaust and of being left without a home at all. That is our story too. The black person who honestly believes 'being anti-Semitic is one way blacks can buy into American life,' has the perception of a flea, and a total ignorance of historically documented, white American behavior. As for those who think the Arab world promises freedom, the briefest study of its routine traditional treatment of blacks (slavery) and women (purdah) will provide relief from all illusion. If Malcolm X had been a black woman his last message to the world would have been entirely different. The brotherhood of Moslem men —all colors—may exist there, but part of the glue that holds it together is the thorough suppression of women.[1] ("To the Editors" 354)

What the above polemic theorizes is the concept of personal "location," for it is precisely the site of location upon which each woman stands, a particular history and set of circumstances that determine her position in the world, not merely among men of racial nationalities, but also among women. By indicting the "female accomplices" of imperialist men, Walker demands that women accept responsibility for their complicitous desires, their "inability to say no." The ability to travel to different worlds, to empathize and demonstrate solidarity with others, requires an understanding that there is enough on this earth for everyone; Walker suggests that while men may choose to war and divide the land, women must seek to unite the divide and claim the whole for all.

While Walker's ability and the ability of her friend to physically travel to other worlds is as much a matter of social class position as it is an object of theoretical praxis, the ability to travel is relative. For some it may mean an excursion to a different neighborhood or a cross-cultural connection in the workplace. We travel each time we encounter difference in our daily interaction with different cultures/artifacts/persons in public and private spaces and media. And the act of traveling can be borne on the winds and waves of imagination. For example, a practice of reading literature that consciously desires to experience the interconnections among women across differences—that is, that desires a transnational feminism—can be nurtured by a transnational feminist writing practice which demonstrates those kinds of human bonds. In her novel *Meridian,* published in 1976, Walker imagines the cross-cultural paradigm that becomes her signature in later novels.

In *Meridian* the concept of "world traveling" is demonstrated in the preoccupation of Walker's characters with Native American history and the family's Indian bloodline. Because Meridian (Walker's African American protagonist), her father, and Feather-Mae, Meridian's great-grandmother, possess a spiritual connection to the Georgia Cherokee, Walker invites her readers to consider a Native American perspective and a shared Native American–African American experience of U.S. colonialism. Meridian's father is painfully conscious of the fact that he currently lives on land once inhabited by the Cherokee. He journeys to their world through family memories, maps, historical documents, and a strong sense of shared space. This act of "world traveling" does not require that the character leave home, for what he travels to is not a place in the world but a Native American cosmos.

Even Meridian's very name carries the history of the interconnections between Native Americans and African Americans, as Melba Joyce Boyd points out in her essay "Politics of Cherokee Spirituality in Alice Walker's *Meridian.*" Boyd constructs a signifying chain of literary and historical references to this connection based on Walker's choice of name for her protagonist. Boyd first invokes Jean Toomer's long poem "The Blue Meridian" (1936), which envisions the destruction of the barrier of race between the African, European, and indigenous peoples of America and the birth of a new people united in spirit. She then visits Margaret Walker's poem "For Andy Goodman—Michael Schwerner—and James Chaney," which proclaims these three slain Civil Rights workers to be Meridians, transcendent beings with the "dignity of a sequoia," which Boyd reads as the Cherokee scholar Sequoia (qtd. in Boyd 16). The commitment of Meridian to experiencing her Native American ties by making a pilgrimage to Merida, a region of the Yucatán, forms the third link in this chain. It is in Merida, whose Mayan inhabitants were called Meridians, that the protagonist shares her great-grandmother's spiritual vision cementing her relationship to the native peoples of the

Americas and to the Cherokee, specifically. Boyd notes that "Indian migration into the Southeastern region of North America was a consequence of Mayans fleeing Aztec tyranny" (20).

This shared history of displacement ties the indigenous peoples of North America to diasporic Africans and reappears in a brief reference in *The Color Purple*. In *Purple*, Nettie writes to Celie of the Trail of Tears, the forced march through winter snows which led those Cherokees who survived it away from their homes in Georgia to resettlement camps in Oklahoma. And it is through Nettie's' letters to her sister Celie that we see Walker begin to articulate her ideas about the identity fragmentation that results from displacement from one's metaphoric and actual home. Walker's reference here also acts as a revelation of autobiographical fragmentation, since she herself claims both African American and Native American heritage. By demonstrating the similar histories of displacement shared by African Americans and Native Americans resulting from the encounter with Europeans, Walker creates the opportunity for all displaced peoples to connect across national boundaries based upon common experience. Hence, for Walker, transnational feminism is not merely the ability to visit the world of others but also to see ourselves in the experience of others and to see them in ours.

THE COLOR PURPLE

Walker's cross-cultural imagining arrives at a substantial level of maturity in the novels she produced in the 1980s and 1990s, beginning with her re-visioning of the colonial project in Africa in *The Color Purple*. By revisiting the identity issues of race, class, gender, and nationality as Walker constructs them in *The Color Purple*, we can identify a developing postcolonial, transnational feminist writing practice. But Walker is not, in every instance, even-handed in considering the identity politics of her characters and their circumstances. In her later novels Walker revisions the world in an acritical way where social economic class is concerned. Walker's level of class consciousness is keen in her recollections of her visit to Cuba: the advantages of a classless society can be summed up in the potential of such a society to eliminate dehumanizing forms of social antagonism. However, the world Walker often creates in much of her fiction is a utopian fantasy in which the characters are granted privileges unattained by her own father, offering no satisfactory explanation of how these worlds evolve from the one we know, an often dehumanizing class system.

The Color Purple depicts the cultural manifestations of oppression, the patriarchal family, and the colonial state, but only indirectly indicts the material or economic motivations of social reproduction. Walker's choice of the epistolary form for this novel indicates that the focus of the story will be on the individual, the letter writer, her struggle within the patriarchal family, and situates that struggle in a broader social and historical concern for literacy. The fragmenting effect of the constant starting and stopping forces the reader to supply transitions to occupy the gaps between letters, effectively drawing the reader into Celie's journey of self-discovery. The importance of Celie's ability to write her own history becomes clear from the outset.

Initially, Celie writes out of shame to the only audience allowed her, God. Her Pa's invective that "You'd better never tell nobody but god; it'd kill your Mama" prevents her from seeking protection from his sexual abuse from the primary source who should be responsible for protecting her, her mother. Celie begins to address her letters to Nettie when it becomes clear to her that "God" is either not listening or has no interest in the fact that she has been traded to Mr. _____, who continues to abuse her physically and mentally, and who separates her from her beloved sister. She has no real knowledge of where to send the letters, however, as she does not know Nettie's fate after she was forced to leave the house Celie keeps for Mr. _____. Yet Celie continues to write.

In his chapter, "Color Me Zora," comparing Walker's *The Color Purple* to Zora Neale Hurston's *Their Eyes Were Watching God,* Henry Louis Gates asserts that this need to write about one's life experiences, even in the absence of the intended reader, is crucial to the development of a sense of consciousness. While Hurston frames her novel as an oral storytelling act where Janie, the protagonist, recalls her life experiences and reveals what she has learned about herself to her friend Phoeby, Walker "represents Celie's growth of self-consciousness as an act of writing." While Janie speaks herself into being, "Celie, in her letters, writes herself into being" (Gates, *Signifying Monkey* 243). Hurston's framing drops away once we enter the story: "free indirect discourse overtakes the narrative," and we lose the immediacy of Janie's narration (251). But Walker's choice of the epistolary form prevents this kind of distance from Celie as a character determined to tell her own story in a manner that allows her to "read the text of her life as the events unfold" (245). Not only are we aware that the narrative voice is Celie's, but we must encounter all the other voices (characters) of the story through her writing. Even Nettie's letters to Celie are arranged, introduced, and commented upon by Celie. However, bell hooks sees Walker's epistolary method in a different light. In "Reading and Resistance: *The Color Purple*," she states: "Functioning as a screen, the letters keep the reader at a distance, creating the illusion of intimacy where there is none. The reader is always voyeur, outsider looking in, passively awaiting the latest news" (294). But I maintain that it is Walker's use of this literary form that signals an intent to tell a story of one woman's struggle for self-definition and which creates a sense of immediacy allowing Walker to demonstrate through Celie the self-reflective impulse we have found also in her essays.

Celie's own story of incest, of being the object of exchange between Pa and Mr. _____, of continued physical and mental abuse at Mr. _____'s hands, and of her love of and redemption through Shug, the blues singer who has long been the object of Mr. _____'s love, form the foundation for the narrative Celie writes about herself. Yet intertwined with Celie's self-sorting is another narrative of oppression. It is in the subtext, Nettie's letters to Celie from Africa, and in the indirect discourse revealed in one of these letters in particular, that Walker addresses the material realities which support Celie's and Nettie's journeys of self-discovery. In Nettie's letters to Celie, Walker permits her reader to interrogate the missionizing impulse that sends Corrine and Samuel to Africa. And in Nettie's descriptions of African women's experiences in an indigenous patriarchal structure made more reactionary in response to the introduction of Western religion and economic colonialism, we begin to see examples of women's shared oppression on the basis of gender.

The impulse to do missionary work is presented as a problem, almost from the outset. Nettie's desire to learn about Africa, the destination of her benefactors, Samuel and Corrine, and eventually her desire to accompany them are constructed as a kind of escape from the racism of her town. It is when Nettie sees Sophia, serving as a maid to the mayor's wife, and speaks to her only to see her "erase" herself, become a nonbeing rather than acknowledge the depth of her own subjugation, that Nettie becomes interested in reading about Africa. She is unable to find a job in town, and caring for Corrine and Samuel's children in Africa seems her best alternative. But the Missionary Society of New York, which is to fund their effort, and the Anti-Slavery and Missionary Society in England are drawn in less than sympathetic terms, even through Nettie's inexperienced eyes. The New York organization does not "say anything about caring about Africa, but only about duty" (*Purple* 127). The British seem clearer on the proper role of missionaries "because the English have been sending missionaries to Africa and India and China and God knows where all, for over a hundred years" (129). In England Nettie sees museums "packed with jewels, furniture, fur carpets, swords, clothing, even *tombs*" from their "host" countries (129). And in England Nettie learns that Africa has "fallen on hard times," which, despite the forgetfulness of these English missionaries, Nettie attributes to the "slave catching wars" and the international slave trade.

Even as Nettie expresses Samuel's vision of their own work as African American missionaries in Pan-Africanist terms—working for the "uplift of black people everywhere"—Walker reveals their missionary work as an example of the complicity of diasporic Africans with European colonialism in the exploitation of indigenous African people (127). En route to their mission, Corrine, Samuel, and Nettie pass through Monrovia, "an African country that was 'founded' by ex-slaves from America" (129). Nettie notes that the president is a "white-looking colored" man and that his cabinet contains many men who look like him as well as some Europeans. She recalls his use of the term "native" to refer to the original inhabitants who now work the "cacao plantations" and notes their absence from the president's cabinet. Corrine explains to her that not even the ruling class of repatriated Africans control the economic base, but people "in a place called Holland . . . who make Dutch chocolate" (132).

In relating the ravages of economic colonialism among the Olinka people, Walker's text prepares us for Samuel's self-critical analysis of the missionary project. The road that has been approaching the Olinka village arrives at and proceeds right through the village, destroying yam fields, the church, the mission school, and Nettie's hut. The villagers are stunned to learn that the whole territory is now owned by an English rubber manufacturer. African people from other villages are employed to topple ancient forests which were the hunting ground, to plow under food crops and the Olinka's source of roofing material; the land is forced to "lie flat" so that it might be planted in rubber trees. The Olinka no longer own their land, and are forced to pay rent for it and tax for their use of water. As this is the only area in the vicinity with a supply of fresh water, the rubber company claims their village and displaces the Olinka to arid ground which cannot be easily tilled, forcing them to purchase water from the rubber company. Barracks are constructed for the rubber plantation workers, but as the indigenous roofing material has been destroyed, the village must buy corrugated tin to cover the barracks.

Upon returning to England to protest the Olinka's treatment, Nettie and Samuel begin to suspect the enormity of the English colonial project. With the approach of World War II, Africa and other colonies provided a source of lumber for ships and land for the cultivation of raw materials for manufactured goods. When the Missionary Society proves to be more interested in the personal relationship between Nettie and Samuel than in hearing their concerns on behalf of the Olinka, Samuel suggests that they return to Africa and urge the Olinka to join the *mbeles,* the "forest people, who live deep in the jungle, refusing to work for whites or be ruled by them" (203). But Nettie realizes how deeply entrenched are the tentacles of European capital:

> But suppose they do not want to go? I asked. Many of them are too old to move back into the forest. Many are sick. The women have small babies. And then there are the youngsters who want bicycles and British clothes. Mirrors and shiny cooking pots. They want to work for the white people in order to have these things. (207)

And yet, while Walker attempts to provide the material motive for Africa's predicament under colonialism, the material base for the predicament of her U.S.-based middle-class African community (landowners, entrepreneurs, and artists) is scarcely mentioned. The historical and material grounding of *The Color Purple*'s U.S. setting depends upon the reader's knowledge of broader historical circumstance. Through indirect discoveries later in the novel, the economic motives behind the death of Celie's natural father are presented almost as an appendage to Samuel's revelation, related in one of Nettie's letters, that "Pa not pa" (163).

Lauren Berlant, in "Race, Gender, and Nation in *The Color Purple,*" suggests that the revelation that Celie and Nettie's "pa" is not their biological father is further complicated by the added knowledge that their real father and his two brothers were lynched by the local white shop owners who felt threatened by their competition and economic success. This second "origin story" shifts the dynamics of Celie's oppression (as well as her identity) from the individual family to the larger community of racial antagonism. It further places the characters Celie and Nettie in a class position which they inherit after "Pa's" death, one which Nettie also achieves through her association with Samuel and Corrine.

Another place in the novel where Walker hints at the material motive of racial oppression is in the story of Sophia, who is farmed out by the local penal system to serve as a domestic servant for the mayor's wife. Sophia's state of peonage is indeed an economic condition and customary in a racial hierarchy and laissez-faire capitalist economy. Sophia is unable to resist sexist and racist oppression in the public sphere. Bell hooks points out that Sophia is regarded as a serious threat to the social order: "Her suffering cannot be easily mitigated as it would require radical transformation of the social order. . . . Sophia's courageous spirit evokes affirmation, even as her fate strikes fear and trepidation in the hearts and minds of those who would actively resist oppression" (hooks, "Reading and Resistance" 290). Hooks's critique of *The Color Purple* is (mis)guided by the notion that the text is a contemporary reworking of the slave autobiography, and while she demonstrates the text's many departures and omissions that distinguish it from the original slave narrative form, hooks' interpretation is haunted by the fact that if this is Walker's intent, it is unacknowledged. Because hooks insists upon calling *The Color Purple* a (failed) contemporary slave narrative, the novel does not fit her definition of revolutionary literature, the goal of which is "education for critical consciousness, creating awareness of the forces that oppress and recognition of the way these forces might be transformed" (292). The slave narrative as revolutionary literature insists that the "individual narrator be linked to the oppressed plight of all black people so as to arouse support for organized political effort for social change" (292).

But whether or not Walker intended to write a contemporary slave narrative, the process of Celie's transformation begs critical examination. Celie's transformation from oppressed object to self-sufficient subject takes place at the level of the individual. At the suggestion of Shug, she adopts the family tradition of small-scale entrepreneurship aided by "Pa's" death and her inheritance of what had been her father's property. As hooks points out, "Walker creates a fiction wherein an oppressed black woman can experience self-recovery without a dialectal process; without collective political effort; without radical change to society" (295). As I will discuss later, privileging private individual transformation in the absence of direct signification of community action is a limitation that Walker overcomes at the end of her later novel *Possessing the Secret of Joy,* where she envisions the interdependence of the two.

Yet Walker's use of cultural Pan-Africanism, her demonstration of self-reflexivity on the part of the African American missionaries, and her suggestion that indigenous patriarchy in the African setting is mirrored by repressive practices in the United States, complicate our reading of

Celie's transformation and provide early manifestations of a transnational feminist consciousness. Walker's characters do not simply travel from one point to another: they encounter as well the "sameness" that affirms their identity as African people. This sense of sameness represents one of the cementing elements of Walker's Pan-Africanism. Nettie writes to Celie not only about the similarities between African (Olinkan) and African American rituals of celebration—picnics include "watermelon, fresh fruit punch, and barbecue"—but also about shared oral literature (154). Nettie describes the friendship between Tashi, one of the Olinka children, and Olivia, Celie's daughter who is being raised by Samuel and Corrine as their child:

> Sometimes Tashi comes over and tells stories that are popular among the Olinka children. I am encouraging her and Olivia to write them down in Olinka and English. It will be good practice for them. Olivia feels that, compared to Tashi, she has no good stories to tell. One day she started in on an "Uncle Remus" tale only to discover Tashi had the original version of it! Her little face just fell. But then we got into a discussion of how Tashi's people's stories got to America, which fascinated Tashi. She cried when Olivia told how her grandmother had been treated as a slave. (152)

Not only does Walker, through Nettie, point to African folklore as the origin for many African American folktales, but she invokes the international slave trade as the medium of exchange and suggests that this connection needs to be recorded by both Africans and African Americans.

And it is through Samuel's Pan-African vision of missionary work that Walker reveals both the anti-imperialist potential of conscious self-critique and the limitations of such potential in this novel. Nettie describes Samuel's eagerness in spite of a less than enthusiastic send-off by the Missionary Society upon their departure for Africa: "Samuel looked a little sad too, but then he perked up and reminded us that there is one big advantage we have. We are not white. We are not Europeans. We are black like the Africans themselves. And that we and the Africans will be working for a common goal: the uplift of black people everywhere" (127). However, from their arrival in Africa, it becomes clear that Samuel's Pan-African construction of race offers little advantage to these missionaries. Nettie describes passing through Senegal, their first stop in Africa, where she sees many more Europeans than she had expected. In the market, the Senegalese "looked through [Nettie and her party] as quickly as they looked through the white French people who live there" (131). Black American missionaries are seen in the same light as European colonials. In several of her letters, Nettie expresses dismay that the African people she meets do not acknowledge these African Americans as children of their country people, refusing to admit to their own participation in the slave trade and to understand why it is that the African American missionaries do not speak their African language or "remember the old ways" (210).

Through Nettie's letters, we understand that she and Samuel have developed "a critical consciousness that allows them to see the connections between Western cultural imperialism and Christianity" (hooks, "Reading and Resistance" 289). Samuel begins to doubt the suitability of the Christian directive of "one husband and one wife" in a culture that practices polygyny which seems to foster very strong female friendships and support networks (*Purple* 153). He and Nettie begin to think of God in a new way: "More spirit than ever before, and more internal" (227). But the inability to prevent the devastation wrought by the rubber plantations elicits from Samuel a critical appraisal of his real position among the Olinka: "They hardly seem to care whether missionaries exist. . . . We love them. We try every way we can to show that love. But they reject us. They never even listen to how we've suffered" (210). When he and Nettie leave Africa to return to the United States, the material life of Olinka has been undermined by colonization; the young people have either become thoroughly appropriated into the colonial economy or have resisted, joined the *mbeles,* and returned to the practices of facial scarification and female genital mutilation that now mark Celie's own family (Adam, Celie's son, and his wife, Tashi). At this juncture in her novel, Walker implicates cultural nationalism as the strategy and ideology of the youth resistance movement, while at the same time implying its impotence in the effort to stop the economic exploitation of the people and the land. Being a Christian missionary, meandering through self-doubt, Samuel has no political ideology or practice, no credibility among the Olinka, with which to strike back at the colonial forces.

The last half of the novel, as we read Samuel and Nettie's disappointment with their lack of success as missionaries, moves the romanticized "Africa" of their imagination to a "space of disappointment and insufficiency" and reveals the limitations of Walker's literary construction of cultural Pan-Africanism based on Christian missionary work (Berlant 226). Her message here concerns the failure of missionary work in Africa, not Pan-Africanism. In the subtext of her next two novels, *The*

Temple of My Familiar and *Possessing the Secret of Joy,* Walker implies the political efficacy of the international Pan-African movement, but, as in her earlier work, bourgeois cultural manifestations of broad political movements are privileged. In these novels, Africa exists in the state of neocolonialism.

While Walker's vision of cultural and racial Pan-Africanism is limited in *The Color Purple,* her critique of indigenous patriarchy among the fictitious Olinka lays the groundwork for her later fiction and documentary film. In Nettie's letters to Celie about the "bit of bloody cutting around puberty," Walker foreshadows the stand she takes in *Possessing the Secret of Joy.* Her criticism of the practice of female genital mutilation sends Walker to Senegal, the Gambia, and Burkina Faso with filmmaker Pratibha Parmar to document the practice and African women's resistance efforts. Reading *The Color Purple* in the context of Walker's later work insists that we perceive the indigenous African patriarchal practices catalogued by Nettie as existing within a much larger system of practices that oppress women and that beg for a transnational feminist analysis.

For instance, Nettie notes the similarities between the patriarchal family structure in which she and Celie grew up and the male-female relations she observes in the Olinka:

> There is a way that men speak to women that reminds me too much of Pa. They listen just long enough to issue instructions. They don't even look at women when women are speaking. . . . The women also do not "look in a man's face" as they say. To "look in a man's face" is a brazen thing to do. . . . [I]t is our own behavior around Pa. (149)

Even as a child, Olivia is capable of perceiving similar power dynamics between patriarchal practices among the Olinka and U.S. racism: Nettie writes "Why can't Tashi come to school? she asked me. When I told her the Olinka don't believe in educating girls she said, quick as a flash, They're like white people at home who don't want colored people to learn" (145). The traditional patriarchy that disempowers Olinkan girls occupies the same position as the racial hierarchy that disempowers black Americans. The connection between patriarchal practices and colonial domination is further sutured by Nettie's description of Tashi's parents' concern for her welfare if she is allowed to continue attending the mission school. While Tashi performs her required domestic tasks and adeptly learns the lessons of female Olinkan practice, her mother fears that "this knowledge does not really enter her soul" (148). Tashi "is becoming someone else; her face is beginning to show the spirit of one of her aunts who was sold to the trader because she no longer fit into village life. This aunt refused to marry the man chosen for her. Refused to bow to the chief" (148). Western education is feared as the impetus to the destruction of traditional gender roles, but at the same time, it is the colonial network that provides punishment for Tashi's aunt's refusal to live within her prescribed cultural parameters. The "trader on the coast" has historic and economic relevance as one of the major linchpins in the encounter between European nations and their would-be colonies (149). In giving her characters the ability to connect their experiences across national constructions—*la facultad*—Walker establishes the "sameness" that serves as a basis for transnational collective action, although it is not until later, in *Possessing,* that we see substantive evidence of this potential.

This inherent capacity for communal response to oppression is contained in *The Color Purple,* however, by the manner in which Walker concludes the novel. Lauren Berlant points to the final scene as being symbolic of how the novel fails to realize its radical potential. Celie is reunited with her children and sister at Celie's newly inherited home and store, the base of operations for her Folkpants, Unlimited. Celie's last letter is addressed to God and expresses her thankfulness for the reconstruction of her family, and describes the reunion as a Fourth of July celebration, a celebration which Berlant calls "American nationalism at its most blatant" (230). Berlant goes on to suggest that "to enter, as the novel does, into a mode of political analysis that employs the ideological myths of hegemonic culture to define Afro-American cultures raises questions about the oppositional status of the novel. . . . [T]he novel . . . represents the mythic spirit of American capitalism as the vehicle for the production of an Afro-American utopia" (232, 233). The idea that capitalism, which has provided the motive force for the disenfranchisement of the black community, can be a viable tool for black women's liberation and national reconstruction reveals the uncritical eye of the author and leaves the success of the novel dependent upon its ability to generate the cultural manifestations of economic and social domination intimated in the unexplored story of Celie and Nettie's real father.

In *The Color Purple,* Walker's engagement of the colonial project and her collision with traditional patriarchy indirectly evoke the materialist subtext. My chapter resolves Walker's indirect discourse with a class analysis. Luce Irigaray's discussion of the traffic in women among men in patriarchal culture, a discussion that will be revisited later in this chapter, reveals how the homosocial exchange of women (as between Pa and Mr. _____) facilitates the reproduction of social relationships born out of notions of property rights and the distribution of material wealth in these cultures. A theory of the social organization of differential material well-being that explains the relations between the customs of patriarchal culture and the economic imperatives of domination of women by men, and that sees the relations of gender as part of the larger project of the exploitation of groups by other groups and of nations by other nations, renders new insights into the writings of Alice Walker. This kind of analysis allows a reading of Walker's *The Color Purple, The Temple of My Familiar,* and *Possessing the Secret of Joy* that will reveal the position of women in patriarchal society, both modern and traditional, and the complicity of patriarchy in the practice of economic exploitation and the systematic production and reproduction of economic relations.

THE TEMPLE OF MY FAMILIAR

The Temple of My Familiar, the second in Walker's trilogy of Pan-Africanist novels, occupies an especially important place in Walker's later fiction. In this novel Walker attempts to present native African characters as representative of whole human beings; they speak, have politics, and overcome private dilemmas. *Temple* thus begins the process of creating a voice for Walker's African characters, although this process arrives at its full bloom with Tashi in *Possessing the Secret of Joy. Temple* is a postmodernist fiction that represents identity fragmentation in light of its resilience. The characters in the novel are cosmopolitan in their outlook; Walker is clearly rejecting a cultural nationalism that thwarts individual self-exploration and the possibility of cross-cultural identity construction, and she offers a counternarrative to patriarchal relations of marriage and family afforded to her characters based upon their privileged position in the Babylon of Western civilization. But while the resolution of the novel's main characters' interpersonal relationships depends, in part, on their privileged economic status, *Temple* insistently links private and public struggle and begins to lay the groundwork for the kind of collective action that is the "resolution" of *Possessing.*

    The Temple of My Familiar traces the lives and past lives of several characters, most through their various relationships with Suwello, a history teacher who returns to Baltimore after the death of his uncle to bring closure to his uncle's affairs. This process, however, brings him in contact with Lissie and Hal, the remaining two members of his Uncle Rafe's close-knit family. Lissie's and Hal's personal narratives prompt Suwello's own self-examination and initiate his emotional transformation. While Suwello is the thread who loosely connects the many lives of this novel, it is mainly the character of Lissie who offers insight into Walker's method and theory of transnational feminism. In *Temple,* Walker's method is mythmaking, and this myth is delivered most directly by Lissie. (In an indirect way, Walker performs her mythmaking through the creation of a petit bourgeois, postmodern utopia inhabited by the U.S. subjects at the conclusion of the novel, a condition I will address at a later point.) Through creating past lives which Lissie remembers and relates, Walker creates a mythic re-visioning of female empowerment and the encroachment of patriarchy; Walker "conjures" an originary narrative to explain the inception of patriarchal societal relations and racial difference.

In relating one of her incarnations, Lissie reveals the roots of patriarchal religion:

> They burned us so thoroughly we did not even leave smoke. . . . The first witches to die at the stake were the daughters of the Moors. . . . It was they (or, rather, we) who thought the Christian religion that flourished in Spain would let the Goddess of Africa "pass" into the modern world as "the Black Madonna." After all, this was how the gods and goddesses moved from era to era before, though Islam, our official religion for quite a long time by now, would have nothing to do with this notion; instead, whole families in Africa who worshiped the Goddess were routinely killed, sold into slavery, or converted to Islam at the point of the sword. . . . Our poor fathers, whose only crime was that they loved their Mother . . . in seeking to protect Her and themselves, helped to change us all, finally, into another spirit and another race. . . . The Inquisitors slaughtered our fathers and took their property for the church. . . . They said the mother of their white Christ (blonde, blue-eyed, even in black-headed Spain) could never have been a black woman, because both the color black and the female sex were of the devil. We were evil witches to claim otherwise. (194–96)

In this version of the Spanish Inquisition, Walker-Lissie links the destruction of matriarchal religion to the establishment of white racial supremacy in medieval Europe.

The myth of these "Motherworshippers," revealed in another of Lissie's remembered lives, indicts the slave trade as a conductor of both racial domination and patriarchal entrenchment. In this incarnation, Lissie recalls that after the death of her father, her uncle sold her, her siblings, and their mother to slave traders. In the slave fort to which they had been brought to be prepared for the Middle Passage and a life of enslavement, Lissie realizes that these "Motherworshippers" comprise large numbers of the men sold to slavers at that time. But even for "hundreds of years previous to the slave trade," the "ancient tradition of worship of the mother" had been under attack:

> There were raids on the women's temples . . . with the women and children dragged out by the hair and forced to marry into male-dominated tribes. . . . The men had decided they would be creator, and they went about dethroning woman systematically. To sell women and children for whom you no longer wished to assume responsibility or to sell those who were mentally infirm or who had in some way offended you, became a new tradition, an accepted way of life. As did the idea, later on, under the Mohametans, that a man could own many women, as he owned many cattle or hunting dogs. (63–64)

Lissie identifies "the hundreds of years of the slave trade in Africa" as the final destruction of this religion that worshipped a female deity (63).

In Walker's myth, patriarchy is even older than the slave trade or the appearance in Africa of Islam. And like the slave trade, patriarchal domination is rooted in the appropriation of human property, this act of appropriation being inevitably the exclusive right of white males to own and have power over women. In a "prehistory" life, Lissie thus links the establishment of a male-dominated social structure and the foundation of capitalist relations. In this story, Lissie remembers being a lion, the "familiar" of a young woman and her children:

> We grew up together and frequently shared our favorite spots in the forest, or stared by night into the same fire. But this way of life was rapidly ending, for somehow or other by the time I was fully grown, the men's camp and the women's had merged. And they had both lost their freedom to each other. The men now took it on themselves to say what should and should not be done by all . . . and the women . . . now became emotionally dependent on the individual man by whom man's law now decreed they must have all their children. . . . [T]he men asserted themselves, alone, as the familiars of women. (364–65)

The condition of male proprietorship and female subjugation under patriarchal monogamous marriage emerges in reciprocal relation to capitalism: the exclusive ownership and control of human labor exercised on the female body. Before this period during which the female and male societies merge and men become dominant, Lissie relates another stage in Walker's re-visioning of social evolution. Lissie remembers being a young man who grows up with his mother's "tribe" and who, according to custom, seeks a mate at the appropriate time. Custom demands that, after mating, the young man is then allowed to go live with the male social group and the young woman raises her child with the help of the female community, perhaps choosing to mate again. Through his intended mate, however, this young man whom Lissie remembers being discovers that the berry-and-nut-based ointment that his mother has been applying to his skin has hidden the fact that his skin is white. This albino is exiled from the human community and cared for only by his mother's "familiar," a lion who has been his mother's constant companion. The lion brings him the skin of a fresh kill so that he may cover his "nakedness," but wearing an animal skin further alienates him from the local animals, who, until that point, had no reason to fear humans. In one stroke of a pen, Walker manages to imagine the creation of the white race and their estrangement from the natural world of other animals. The lion "familiar" serves as a point of connection between Lissie's final two stories in the novel. Through Lissie, Walker creates an originary myth that links the very beginnings of racial difference, the institution of monogamy through patriarchal social structures, and the establishment of private property.

Myth also functions in Walker's text to indict religious institutions for their suppression of matriarchal religious forms and to connect women cross-culturally in terms of their oppression in male-dominated social formations. Science fiction author Ursula K. Le Guin, in her review of *Temple,* sees Walker's literary creation of "prehistoric lives, Africa of the human dawn, lovingly and fearfully imagined" (23), in the context of a developing female literary tradition:

> So many women are writing such imaginations now that it is surely a communal undertaking responding to a communal need. . . . [W]omen are studying such societies in a radical and subversive effort to think back to before things went wrong. . . . [This endeavor] takes a long mental journey, and a hard one, since the evidence of what went before white patriarchy has been systematically defiled and destroyed. But the women writing these books are going back so we can go forward. (23–24)

Lissie moves over time, across cultures, races, and sexes: she is a true "world traveler." Lissie represents our potential to move beyond essential identities. Maria Lugones suggests that the best way to develop "loving perception" of those who occupy different communities from us is to "travel" to those "worlds" and to see who *we* are through *their* eyes. Lissie is Walker's literary embodiment of this kind of feminist theory. Lissie's travels offer us an opportunity to consider alternative (albeit prehistoric) gender relations and the destructive tendencies of patriarchy. Similarly, Walker uses other characters in the novel who, like Lissie, travel between worlds. With these characters, Walker shifts from myth, in the ancient sense, to ideology ("myth" in the modern sense).

The act of traveling for these other characters in *Temple* is not one of time traveling, as in the case of Lissie, but rather a kind of travel that is politically charged. Walker's anticolonial-neocolonial discourse is facilitated by the ability of her characters to move between worlds (geographic locations) as agents of ideology and political warfare. Because Zedé, a university-educated teacher in an unnamed South American country, for example, appears to us as an ethnoscape, in Arjun Appadurai's sense, we are invited as readers to engage an anticolonial discourse in which Zedé is not only an agent against neocolonial subjugation but also a conductor of a postmodern, postcolonial underground railroad. As a conductor, she is a character who travels to a different world and who therefore allows us as readers to be her traveling companions.

The novel opens with the story of Zedé, who finds herself incarcerated as a Communist when the school in which she is teaching is closed by the fascist government. After the murder of her lover, a member of the resistance, she escapes and finds a job as a "maid-servant" in a "school" that "rehabilitates" drug-addicted children of the international elite. At this school, where her daughter Carlotta is born, Zedé meets Mary Ann Haverstock, a young woman from the United States whose parents have placed her in this institution because of her use of drugs and her predilection for political radicals who tended to take advantage of her incoherent state to get at the very sizable fortune of her parents. Zedé comes to realize that the "school" is simply a front of the corporate neocolonial bourgeoisie; the young people who reside there are locked up and tranquilized, receiving no treatment for drug dependency or emotional disorders, while the parents are charged dearly for its "services." Zedé grows to like Mary Ann and writes covertly to her parents alerting them to the true conditions of the school and advising them to retrieve their daughter.

After Mary Ann is rescued she returns, working with the resistance, to free Zedé and Carlotta and bring them to the United States. During the process, Mary Ann stages her death, becomes Mary Jane Briden, and surfaces later in the novel in the village of Olinka (of Walker's *The Color Purple*). Like the character Zedé, whom we witness traveling between California and South America, Mary Ann/Jane is also a world traveler, and we become acquainted with her through the device of Zedé's travel narrative. Mary Jane (now Miss B), in the tradition of her great-great-aunt Eleandra, who rescued and returned to Africa an Ababa woman (sister tribe to the Olinka) who had been living as an exhibit in the British Museum of Natural History, lives among the Olinka. Funded by what she has managed to salvage from her parents' fortune, Miss B operates an art school, which is dedicated to the rehabilitation of parentless young people of Olinka who suffer the physical and emotional scars of the war for independence that orphaned them. To a lesser degree than Zedé, Mary Ann/Jane (Miss B) also functions as a conductor in Walker's narrative. Through her travels we are allowed to visit the Olinka; however, once arriving at this new location, she becomes the by-product of the playwright Ola's story. We identify with her as a subject in an indirect discourse.

It is indirectly, through Ola's part of Walker's narrative, that Miss B functions to raise the issue of how best to deal with the former colonizing and expatriated population, often deeply entrenched in the economy and day-to-day operations of the newly independent African nation. Because Miss B's mission is constructed as a genuinely altruistic one, Walker marries her off to Ola, minister of culture for the now-independent Olinka, solely for the purpose of avoiding her exclusion from the country with other non-African property owners. The political significance of their marriage does not stop at this, however. Through his marriage to Miss B, Ola uses the nationalist government's return to polygyny to challenge their own preservation of the colonial government's ban of interracial marriage. The circumstances that draw together Miss B, Ola, and his two daughters, one African (Nzingha) and one African American (Fanny), represent Walker's concern in this novel for the role of the cultural worker in the process of decolonization in Africa and the ways in which non-Africans can support this process.

That Ola is a playwright rather than a novelist, for example, is no mere coincidence:

> [M]ore than the other literary arts, drama deals at a highly concentrated, more intense level with the contradictions of social existence. A

dramatic piece which does not, in one form or another, deploy as its organising structural criterion, a physical or emotional conflict, a moral or spiritual contest of wills, a confrontation between contending principles, is almost inconceivable. (Jeyifo 7)

In "A Paradigm for a Radical Sociology of African Drama," Biodun Jeyifo suggests that drama does not simply use conflict as an "organising structural motif" but instead attempts to suggest a resolution of conflict. While Jeyifo warns that cultural (ethnic) and national particularity must be a part of any literary analysis, at the same time "there are great affinities of ideological and cultural expressions which derive from the common historical situation of most African countries as previously colonially subjugated societies, and in the common aspirations of the African peoples to win genuine independence from imperialist domination and to resume the course of self-directed development" (8). The ways in which the central conflict in African drama, in particular, is or is not resolved constitute Jeyifo's "sociology" of African drama and reveal the significance of Walker's choice to create a man of the theater as her representative of the cultural arm of the African struggle to decolonize. Ola's plays suggest both local and Pan-African solutions to neocolonial conflicts.

Ola fought, with Nzingha's mother, as a guerrilla in the war for independence; following the war, because he had been partially educated in Western ways by the missionaries, Ola was sent to Sweden to complete his studies. But as a playwright and minister of culture in the new government, Ola is often silenced and sometimes imprisoned by the nationalist forces. His plays, which frequently attack the elitism of this new government—its unwillingness to move quickly to provide the people fair wages, health care, and accessible schools for their children—are still frequently banned. The content of these plays, and Ola's expressed ideas about the function of drama in political struggle, resemble Jeyifo's progressive political engagement in drama and suggest Walker's theory of cultural activism. Ola, by virtue of his Western education and resulting administrative position in the neocolonial government, is part of the "emergent national petty-bourgeois class" (Jeyifo 47). "Almost to a man," the African playwrights of this period are from this class and are either "in love with, disillusioned with or up in arms against their class" (47). It is clear that Ola is created in this last image. One of his earlier plays, *The Fee,* attacks the new government for neglecting the social and educational welfare of its own working people, while funding an internal military presence with their tax dollars. Fanny, Ola's African American daughter, sees the play produced by students in London and notes that it is "the kind of play no playwright in America would write and that no producer would produce" despite the fact that "everyone there cries about taxes" (*Temple* 159). Further evidence of Ola's dedication to a class analysis can be found in Miss B's revelations about his play that he is rehearsing at the time of his death. This play focuses on the Olinka middle class who, "with the government's blessing, are permitting the country to grow as divided along class lines as it was under the whites along color lines" (347).

While the content of Ola's plays, as described by various characters, makes it clear that he stands "up in arms against" his class, it is in the play about Nzingha's mother that we can read his concern with the responsibility of the postindependence society to women and of the African individual to his or her society. In this play, Ola condemns the lack of female representation in the current government, insisting that "the people," whose armed struggle resulted in the installation of this government, include women as well as men. Using his own disavowal of his wife (with whom he seems to no longer have anything in common) as a self-critique, Ola forces the audience to question their own positions in this postindependence period. Nzingha relates the response of the audience: "They were seeing themselves, in my father's play, for the first time as they more or less were, without the patina of revolution, the slogans of imperialism," suggesting the need for a new ideological framework that does not depend solely upon a common enemy—colonial rule (*Temple* 259).

The question of where to go from here and what part the theater should play in nationbuilding is the subject of a discussion between Ola and two government representatives. Ola is in jail following the bulldozing of the theater where his play is being performed. While these representatives urge Ola to write plays about "people who are trying hard to make something of the country now that the white man has left," Ola replies, "THE WHITE MAN IS STILL HERE. Even when he leaves, he is not gone" (181). The government agents suggest appropriate subject matter would be the colonials' destruction of the white university, radio station, and hospitals rather than leave them for the use of the African population. Ola resists: "EVERYONE ALL OVER THE WORLD KNOWS EVERYTHING THERE IS TO KNOW ABOUT THE WHITE MAN. That's the essential meaning of television. BUT THEY KNOW NEXT TO NOTHING ABOUT THEMSELVES" (182). The real issue for Ola is to move past working against the colonial presence and to find a way to best utilize, in the service of the people, those remnants of Africa's colonial period which cannot be purged.

This exchange demonstrates Walker's concern for the function of the cultural worker in the African setting. Jeyifo suggests that "there is a 'culture' which thrives on and may sustain neo-colonialism and one which radically contests it and defines a revolutionary reconstruction" (Jeyifo 49). The Olinka officials urge the playwright to celebrate their good work despite the years of colonial oppression, a type of cultural production that would "sustain" neocolonialism and a form of cultural work that they promise would "thrive." But Ola continues to "contest" government practices that prevent a "revolutionary" national reconstruction.

In this exchange between Ola and the government agents, Walker raises the issue of gender equity in her critique of the neocolonialism of postindependence Africa. When Ola suggests that the way to proceed with nation building is first through self-examination, the government officials tell him that no one else thinks the way he does. Ola responds that "THE WOMEN THINK AS I DO," to which these petty bureaucrats reply, "WHO CARES WHAT WOMEN THINK" (*Temple* 182). This response haunts the text, and with Ola's death Walker suggests that decolonization is only a beginning. Miss B recalls that Ola had realized "how endless struggle is. . . . [I]t is like the layers of an onion, and smelly, too. . . . [E]ach time he sat down to write a play he was surprised, and a bit disheartened, to see he'd simply arrived at a new layer of stinking suffering that the people were enduring" (347). Removing whites from control of the Olinka government did not represent "the last of their work to insure a prosperous future for their country, instead, it had proved only a beginning" (347). After his death, it is left to Ola's two daughters, Fanny Nzingha, daughter of Olivia (also of *The Color Purple*), who lived as a child in Olinka, and Nzingha, daughter of the freedom fighter and, like her father, an employee of the department of culture, to address the situation of women in Olinka. The "two Nzinghas" turn to the weapon of struggle their father knew best, the African theater.

Rightly conceived, community theater represents a step in the direction of a collective model of struggle. It directly engages people in numbers, though not to the degree of television. It is one of the tools available to revolutionary cultural workers, who usually do not control electronic mass media, and gives them access to numbers of people for consciousness raising. Having suggested, though not thoroughly explored, the potential of the coalition of indigenous African and African American women as a powerful force in the struggle against neocolonial patriarchy, the focus of Walker's novel shifts from Africa to the United States.

This encounter with Africa as a neocolonial condition as Walker describes it in *Temple* is an appeal to the conscience of her reading public to be ever vigilant in the struggle against all forms of domination, including but not limited to racism. Walker suggests here that class and gender oppression must also be resisted and that struggle is a never-ending process. The theoretical groundings of this reading of Walker's narrative resound Chela Sandoval's concept of "differential oppositional consciousness," as Walker's characters seem to engage a balancing and juggling act of multiple subjectivities. Her South American and African protagonists are not merely racial categories: they are not culturally stagnant, but rather hybrids of postcoloniality. Their ability to move between worlds and to join with the inhabitants of those worlds manifests Walker's theory of political and cultural activism. That such a construction is rendered in a literary expression is not without precedent. In *Temple,* Walker alerts the reader to the ongoing resistance against human subjugation in the era of postmodernity and postcoloniality in the same way that the U.S. slave narrative called attention to the institution of bondage in the antebellum period. She appeals to our *la facultad* and invites us to the "joining."

However, it is in the United States that Walker's method of myth dilutes the broader political potential of *Temple*. Being myth, Walker's method fails to render a revolutionary collective process by which communities attain some measure of salvation from the oppressive systems of patriarchy, colonialism, and capitalism. For example, we are not given a pragmatic explanation of how whole communities achieve the utopian vision with which Walker concludes her novel. In this conclusion, the now adult Carlotta has resigned from her university teaching job and become a "bell chimist," living in the guest house on her musician-husband's property in the Berkeley hills. While he is primary caregiver to their children and maintains an open door policy toward her coming and going, the privacy of Carlotta's living space is assured by a system of bells and chimes. Suwello has also resigned from teaching and is writing a book based upon his discussions with Lissie and Hal. With his ex-wife Fanny (Nzingha), now a massage therapist, he is building a house "like a bird" with a separate wing for each of them and some common space in between.

Similarly, the political potential in Walker's South American theater is diluted with a vision of alternative spirituality. Walker seems to abandon her concern for the resistance movement, returns Zedé to her shaman-mother in South America, marries her to a shaman, and leaves them all walking on the beach with the occasional visitor, the once estranged Carlotta. The two Zedés, mother and daughter, return to the traditional cultural work of creating feathered garments for ritual use. As with her U.S. characters, Walker attenuates the subversive potential of cultural production with her emphasis on individual self-exploration over collective political action.

In the final analysis, Walker's main characters in the U.S. setting are alienated individuals, more aware of themselves and the pitfalls of repressive relationships—having learned lessons most of us have not—and yet removed, as are all gods and goddesses of the mythical world, from the everyday realities of real people. Like *The Color Purple,* whose final vision is one of a reconstructed extended family supported by virtue of small-scale entrepreneurship (Celie's and her father's), *Temple* concludes with two reunited heterosexual couples whose bourgeois status allows them to live an idealistic compromise between Lissie's prehistoric myth of separate male and female communities and the culturally mandated U.S. nuclear family. While Walker's ancient myth envisions communal alternatives to patriarchal social structures, her contemporary models of gender reconciliation fail to move beyond the arena of the individual. It is only in *Temple*'s African setting that Walker hints at a collective approach to struggle and points us in the direction of her next novel.

POSSESSING THE SECRET OF JOY

As I have suggested, the ability to travel, to experience other worlds, is more than the physical act of relocation but rather the facility to connect with others and to see the world and ourselves from their perspective. But when we give voice to the perspectival experience of others, a complicated question arises around the issue of "authenticity." Walker's leap from the diasporic African self as the principal site of representation in *The Temple of My Familiar* to the African self as the principal site of representation in *Possessing the Secret of Joy* elicits the difficult issue of who has the "authority" to speak for whom. The "rebirth" of Tashi (from *The Color Purple*) in *Possessing* moves the African protagonist to the United States and, by the end of the novel, back to Africa, further suturing the connection between the continent and the diaspora and underscoring the Pan-African development of Walker's later novels. But it is the stand that Alice Walker takes against female genital mutilation[2] in *Possessing the Secret of Joy* that is the catalyst for the controversy, in the Walker criticism, around the debate of authenticity of voice and perspective. The impulse of black cultural nationalism to romanticize what is believed to be "African tradition" (i.e., the cultural practices of some precolonial, mythic "Africa") turns upon itself when it comes to the relationship between African Americans and African cultural realities. This kind of contradiction sometimes pits the black nation against black womanhood both in the diaspora and on the continent. The voices Walker constructs for her African protagonists transmit a discourse that is perceived by some as "anti"-African culture when in fact it is not. Rather, the discourse which Walker constructs is antipatriarchy, that is, against the control and commodification of the female body, and anti-neocolonial, and in the final analysis promotes collective action against the patriarchal, neocolonial state.

Some might suggest that Alice Walker's stance against female genital mutilation has been compromised by Western morality, white feminism, and Marxist ideology, all of these being alien to "Africa" and therefore not legitimate tools for evaluating African culture. This perspective denies the fact that culture is constructed out of the perceived needs of social groups, out of the need for shelter and food: in short, culture derives from the organizing principles of subsistence. It is these organizing principles to which Walker refers in Lissie's myths; Walker re-visions a "prehistory" moment of the original act of patriarchal exchange—protection and respectability in exchange for sexual fidelity. It is also these organizing principles which make Celie the object of exchange between "Pa," who must marry off the eldest daughter first, and Mr. _____, who needs to have a wife to meet his domestic, child care, and sexual needs so that he can be productive. In *Possessing the Secret of Joy,* Tashi's body bears the physical evidence of a long history of female commodification revisited as an anticolonial strategy. When read as a continuing discourse, this trilogy of novels suggests that female circumcision cannot be easily dismissed as mere culture, but rather must be seen as the social expression of the organizing principles for a group's material production and reproduction. Female circumcision, therefore, is a "term" of agreement in the act of exchange. Circumcision as a term of exchange is performed on the female body which has been transformed into a commodity. To dismiss such a viewpoint, by invoking "Western humanism," "feminism," or "Marxism," is to deny the fundamental organizing principles that Walker overtly and covertly emphasizes in her narrative discourse. Walker's transnational feminist writing practice is undergirded by a critique of the patriarchal exchange of women's bodies.

An approach to *Possessing* that identifies female circumcision as a term of exchange also diverts attention from anthropological explanations and justifications of the phenomenon and forces us to see the practice as one of many ways in which the "sex/gender system" under patriarchy attempts to control female sexuality and maintain lines of kinship and inheritance. This system is articulated by Gayle Rubin in her essay "The Traffic in Women: Notes on the 'Political Economy' of Sex." Rubin locates the "domestication" of women within larger social structures, a "political economy of sexual systems," if you will (177). Lévi-Strauss's theory of kinship organizes human sexuality based upon "the incest taboo, obligatory heterosexuality, and an asymmetric division of the sexes" (Rubin 183). The sexual division of labor within a society is not based upon biological ability but serves to "institute a reciprocal state of dependency between the sexes," therefore ensuring some form of the heterosexual family structure (Lévi-Strauss qtd. in Rubin). Rubin goes on to interpret the division of labor by sex as "a taboo against the sameness of men and women . . . dividing the sexes into two mutually exclusive categories . . . exacerbat[ing] biological differences . . . and thereby *creat*[ing] gender" (178). The incest taboo ensures that family will be linked to family through marriage (in some form). The marriage ceremony is the auction block upon which women are formally exchanged in a homosocial relationship between men—between father (or brother) and groom (the trade of women between "pimps" and "johns" is an illicit form of this kind of exchange). But kinship systems "do not merely exchange women. They exchange sexual access, genealogical statuses, lineage names and ancestors, rights and *people*—men, women, and children—in concrete systems of social relationships. These relationships always include certain rights for men, others for women " (177).

While "kinship systems" serve to explain "the culturalization of biological sexuality on the societal level," it is culture that teaches the individual that biological difference manifests in a sinister system of power relations in which male identity acts as the placeholder of sexual/gendered status (Rubin 189). As Rubin defines patriarchal kinship, "the relationship of a male to every other male is defined through a woman. A man is linked to a son by a mother, to his nephew by virtue of a sister, etc. Every relationship between male kin is defined by the woman between them. If power is a male prerogative, and must be passed on, it must go through the woman-in-between" (Rubin 192 n.). Hence, "as long as men have rights in women which women do not have in themselves, the phallus also carries the meaning of the difference between 'exchanger' and 'exchanged,' gift and giver" (Rubin 191).

It is important to remember that this "exchange of women" does not take place in a vacuum. "Sex/gender systems are not ahistorical emanations of the human mind; they are products of historical human activity" (Rubin 204). As Rubin puts it, "Kinship and marriage are always parts of total social systems, and are always tied into economic and political arrangements" (207). Rubin's Marxist approach to female oppression lays bare the economic interest that men have in women within patriarchal social systems. Culture (i.e., kinship systems and the enculturation of biological sexuality) is an effective and tenacious tool in the maintenance of political/economic systems. We must realize, therefore, that even a successful global socialist revolution cannot, by itself, end sexism. Cultural practices that support inequitable positions of men and women in social systems must also come under scrutiny.

Female genital mutilation (FGM) should/can be acknowledged as one of many practices which perpetuate the sex/gender hierarchy through time and across national identities. In *The Hosken Report: Genital and Sexual Mutilation of Females,* Fran Hosken contextualizes FGM among many forms of female sexual repression practiced worldwide. Hosken notes that the labia rings and chastity belts of medieval Europe, and even in the nineteenth century, gave way to "modern" medical practices such as hysterectomy and surgical infibulation as treatment for a prolapsed uterus and clitoridectomy as a means to control female sexual activity and to "cure" masturbation. "From about 1890 through the late 1930s, female circumcision was performed by physicians in the USA" as treatment for measles, melancholia, kleptomania, and hiccups (295). Hosken makes the further point that, for a time, such surgery promised to be as lucrative a business as is the circumcision of male babies on "pseudo-medical" grounds, and as was Dr. James Burt's "vaginal reconstruction" surgery in the mid-1970s, in his Dayton, Ohio, medical practice.[3] With the medicalization of female sexual functioning, the female body serves not only as a medium of exchange in the maintenance of kinship systems but as a potential gold mine for capitalist exploitation.

In *Possessing,* Walker suggests the collusion of U.S. physicians in using female genital mutilation to repress female sexuality. Tashi's African American therapist, Raye, wants her to know that she is not alone. She introduces her to Amy, an older woman from New Orleans, who suffered genital mutilation at the age of six. Her parents, having tried binding her hands and putting hot pepper sauce on her fingers to discourage her sexual self-exploration, asked the family doctor to excise her clitoris. Amy tells Tashi that "even in America a rich white child could not touch herself sexually" (*Possessing* 185). By introducing Amy, Walker refuses to allow the U.S. reader to distance himself or herself from the practice as one that affects only women of other cultures. Resistance to the exploitation of women as a commodity must take place on several fronts, and cultural workers like Alice Walker accept this challenge; her choice to take up the issue of female genital mutilation must be viewed in this context.

Such cultural practices support the trade in women among men by marking women's value as commodity. In "Women on the Market," Luce Irigaray makes the point that as commodities not all women are equal. Woman has no intrinsic value, but "*has value only in that she can be exchanged*" (Irigaray 176). A woman's value on the market depends upon her ability to prove compliance with cultural dictates. The virginal woman "*is pure exchange value.* She is nothing but the possibility, the place, the sign of relations among men. In and of herself, she does not exist; she is a simple envelope veiling what is really at stake in social exchange. In this sense, her natural body disappears into its representative function" (186). The act of female circumcision, as a term of exchange, signifies the "pure" value of the commodified subject: the scar of circumcision is worn like a decal certifying the quality of an exchangeable good. Egyptian physician and cultural worker Nawal El Saadawi makes it clear that, in the Arab world, the condition of "pure" value must be provable:

> Every female Arab child, even today, must possess that very fine membrane called a hymen, which is considered one of the most essential, if not *the* most essential, part of her body. However, the mere existence of the hymen is not in itself sufficient. This fine membrane must be capable of bleeding profusely, of letting out red blood that can be seen as a visible stain on a white bed sheet the night a young girl is married. (25)

El Saadawi articulates the connection between the practice of genital mutilation and the value of a woman's virginity to the men who would exchange her: "Behind circumcision lies the belief that, by removing parts of girls' external genital organs, sexual desire is minimized. This permits a female who has reached the 'dangerous age' of puberty and adolescence to protect her virginity, and therefore her honour, with greater ease" (33). Rites of passage and chastity are culturally compulsive ideological constructions projected on an economic system. "In the final analysis, we can safely say that female circumcision, the chastity belt and other savage practices applied to women are basically the result of the economic interests that govern society" (41).

As Walker suggests, we need not restrict to Arab countries or to Africa our critique of cultural practices that value women as commodities based upon their sexual purity. El Saadawi's implication of the chastity belt indicts European patriarchy as well. The chastity belt is a European icon with a long history signifying sexual purity and functioning as an emblem of exchange value. The concern with sexual purity and exchange value, articulated to the female body, is a discursive practice that can also be read in European master narratives, for example, in Shakespeare's *Much Ado About Nothing*. The respectability of the "heroine" Hero is challenged because of the malicious finagling of a jealous brother (Don John, brother of Don Pedro, patron of the intended groom), and her predicament calls into question the future of her father's estate.

A feminist reading of *Much Ado* can reveal how tenuous is a sex/gender system in which female virginity marks the exchange between men. Unlike Walker's *Possessing,* wherein the female subject is finally vindicated and where that vindication functions as the climax of the text, it is not Hero who is vindicated in *Much Ado* but rather patriarchal respectability which is restored upon the house of Leonato, her father, with the revelation that Hero's purity is intact. Claudio, her groom-to-be, believing that he has seen Hero in her window with another man the night before, reveals her "treachery" the day of their proposed wedding. As Hero is publicly denounced by him and by her own father, she faints and appears to have died. At the suggestion of Friar Francis, Leonato lets the public and especially Claudio think that such is the case, hoping that something will come to light that explains Claudio's claims and Hero's denial of them. But what is at stake here is more than Hero's good name: it is the public honor of Leonato as well. After the malicious plot to disgrace her honor is revealed, Claudio is required to go to what he believes is Hero's tomb, which Claudio calls "the monument of *Leonato,*" and make a very public proclamation of her innocence so that her name, "in death," will not remain dishonored (*Much Ado* 5.3.1, 8, emphasis added). But this act also functions to absolve Leonato of any shame that Hero's alleged (mis)conduct might bestow upon him for his failure to uphold the patriarchal order. The friar's participation in Leonato's staging of Hero's death in *Much Ado About Nothing* also implicates the church in the maintenance of the patriarchy of Renaissance Europe. It is, after all, religion, at the subtextual level of Shakespeare's drama, that is the institutional perpetrator of the sex/gender economy. And like European master narrative, religion ascribes as normal certain behaviors, practices, and arrangements concerning the sexes that function to ensure sexual purity.

The origin of female genital mutilation, for example, is often tied to Islam. Circumcision, however, has no organic relationship to either Islam or the Koran:

> Many people think that female circumcision only started with the advent of Islam. But as a matter of fact it was well known and widespread in some areas of the world before the Islamic era, including in the Arab peninsula. . . . [C]ircumcision of girls . . . was practised in societies with widely varying religious backgrounds, in countries of the East and the West, and among peoples who believed in Christianity, or in Islam, or were atheistic. . . . Circumcision was known in Europe as late as the 19th century, as well as in countries like Egypt, the Sudan, Somaliland, Ethiopia, Kenya, Tanzania, Ghana, Guinea and Nigeria. It was also practised in many Asian countries such as Sri Lanka and Indonesia, and in parts of Latin America. It is recorded as going back far into the past under the Pharaonic Kingdoms of Ancient Egypt, and Herodotus mentioned the existence of female circumcision seven hundred years before Christ was born. (El Saadawi 39–40)

Because the practice of female genital mutilation predates the appearance of Islam in Africa, the high incidence of this practice in Islamic African communities cannot be explained merely as adherence to religious doctrine.[4] Such a position is further contradicted by the fact that "the procedure is not practiced in predominately Islamic countries such as Saudi Arabia, Iraq, the Gulf States, Kuwait, Algeria, and Pakistan" (Toubia 32). The practice of female genital mutilation in Islamic African communities, therefore, reflects the political appropriation of circumcision by the church for the purpose of controlling female sexuality on behalf of a patriarchal ruling class. This collusion of interests exemplifies the "scattered hegemonies" that Grewal and Kaplan identify as the appropriate subject of transnational feminist practice.

And further, it is not only religion that appropriates circumcision for political purposes. The symbolic value of circumcision is not always directly concerned with sexual purity, although it may remain a rite of passage. Such is the case in Walker's *Possessing the Secret of Joy,* where circumcision is politically appropriated by the anticolonial resistance movement as an act of cultural defiance, a mark of Africanism, in response to European imperialism. But Walker's narrative critique of the appropriation of FGM by anticolonial forces raises questions about Africa's national liberation movements that romanticize precolonial African traditions, even those which are reactionary in their treatment of women. Jomo Kenyatta's political appropriation of circumcision as a fundamental part of Kenya's national reconstruction is one example of the wrong-headed embrace of Africa's traditional practices. In *Possessing,* Walker goes as far as to "call Kenyatta out" as she makes direct reference to him: "Our Leader, our Jesus Christ, said we must keep all our old ways and that no Olinka man—in this he echoed the great liberator Kenyatta—would even think of marrying a woman who was not circumcised" (Tashi in *Possessing* 120–21). But not all anticolonial resistance movements construct national culture by uncritically embracing precolonial traditional practices. Alternative models to the kind of national culture espoused by Kenyatta and revisited by Walker in her novel can be seen in the examples of Thomas Sankara, Marxist president of Burkina Faso, who spoke publicly against the practice of female genital mutilation, and in the case of Eritrea, where the Eritrean People's Liberation Front opposed the practice in an effort to recruit more women to the movement for independence.

Political opposition to the practice of female genital mutilation rests squarely on a site of struggle where cultural identity comes into conflict with the well-being of women; this seems to be the reasoning behind the organized effort of continental African women and national liberation movements against the practice. In RAINB♀'s (Research, Action, and Information Network for Bodily Integrity of Women) *Female Genital Mutilation: A Call for Global Action,* published in 1995, Egyptian-born author Nahid Toubia, who served as the first female surgeon in Sudan, points out that "FGM must be separated from the notion that it has a religious basis, while efforts to preserve cultural integrity must be honored. The task will be all the more difficult because individuals and communities are being asked to take action against a longstanding practice that is part of a heritage of which they are proud" (43). Any efforts to organize and speak out against such practices must be "empathic, not alienating. They must recognize all forms of cultural manipulation and mutilation of women's bodies, whether physical or psychological" (43).

Toubia applauds institutional efforts on behalf of women and children on the international level,[5] on the Pan-African level,[6] and on the national level,[7] and calls for public health agencies, international human rights bodies, organizations concerned with women's economic development, and health care and legal workers' professional organizations to develop official positions opposing FGM. But in addition to institutional support, Toubia further calls for constituencies between "teachers, media personnel, artists, singers, writers, actors," utilizing their talents and networks for positive change (Toubia 47). It is within this context that cultural workers such as Alice Walker can stand squarely on the side of women everywhere.

So while "culture" cannot be used to excuse praxis that physically and psychologically harms women and children, any transnational feminist approach to speaking against social practices that perpetrate a sex/gender hierarchy must be able to demonstrate what African American teacher and cultural critic bell hooks calls "authentic solidarity," recognizing (as does Walker) the echoes of these practices in our own cultural settings (*Yearning* 188). For example, hooks recalls having been asked to speak in Toronto at a commemoration of the stand that black South African women took in Pretoria against pass laws. Concerned with the issue of speaking for other women, hooks chose to approach her talk by presenting the points of commonality shared by black women in the United States and South Africa. She relates "memories of growing up in the apartheid black American South, memories of black women leaving the racially segregated spaces of [the] community to work in white homes" (185). Hooks points to a history of de jure and de facto segregation and the experience of gender inequity as points of connection upon which South African and African American women, and all people who are dedicated to militant resistance, can and must struggle. This approach to the act of "speaking for" is evident in Walker's narrative critique of the practice of female genital mutilation.

In her protagonist Tashi, Walker creates a complex, postmodern, postcolonial identity. Rejecting simplistic notions of an immigrant who either embraces her new U.S. culture, or who is bitterly disappointed in discovering the disadvantageous position of a black woman in U.S. society, Walker's Tashi is both and neither: she embraces some aspects and rejects others. Walker enacts multiple and cross-cultural sites of identity even in naming her protagonist; sometimes she is Tashi, sometimes Evelyn (her "American" name), sometimes Tashi-Evelyn or Evelyn-Tashi, and sometimes Mrs. Johnson. Nor is Tashi the nostalgic exile, longing for a romanticized version of home. The thing that sends Tashi home to

Olinka is the desire to avenge her own genital mutilation and the death of her sister at the hands of M'Lissa, the circumciser. But Walker does not allow Tashi's act of murdering the *tsunga,* M'Lissa, to be read simply as an individual act of revenge.

While *Possessing the Secret of Joy* is often read as Walker's critique of female genital mutilation and her examination of the threat it might pose to the individual psyche, the implicit message is one of the necessity of collective resistance. While Tashi is imprisoned during the trial, Olinka women hold a vigil outside her cell, bringing her "wildflowers, herbs, seeds, beads, ears of corn, anything they can claim as their own and that they can spare. . . . Sometimes they sing" (*Possessing* 191). When they commit the audacious act of singing the only song they know in common, the Olinka national anthem of independence, the men, "cultural fundamentalists and Muslim fanatics," attack, kick, and beat the women, who have traveled from all parts of the country to show support for Tashi (191). Along with these demonstrations, some professional Olinka women solicit the neocolonial "president for life" on Tashi's behalf, only to be threatened with the loss of their jobs if they persist (194). Walker even rallies cultural workers and female myth in support of Tashi's position. Olinka female potters visit Tashi's jail cell to present her with a replica of a rediscovered ancient form of sculpture depicting a woman blissfully fondling intact genitals. They suggest that, at one time, these figures were used as "a teaching tool [but] when women were subjugated, these images were sent literally underground, painted on the walls of caves," as current Olinka custom marks such an image as taboo" (197).

While Tashi alone is to be executed for the murder, Walker does not allow even the reader to "know" for certain if Tashi committed the murder, thus inviting the reader to speculate as to who really bears the responsibility of cultural resistance. Tashi denies having done it to Olivia, letting her believe that, in the end, "M'Lissa did die under her own power" (250). But in a letter Tashi writes to the dead Lisette (her husband's lover and mother of his son Pierre, of whom Tashi has grown quite fond) several hours before she is to be executed, Tashi claims that she suffocated M'Lissa before setting fire to her house. Walker's refusal to reconstruct the "murder" for the reader and the widespread support she creates for Tashi among the other Olinka women beg us to read this not as a simple act on the part of an individual but as the collective assault on a cultural institution. The scene Walker creates for the day of Tashi's execution suggests what bell hooks might call a "site of radical possibility, a space of resistance" (*Yearning* 149):

The women along the way have been warned they must not sing. Rock-jawed men with machine guns stand facing them. But women will be women. Each woman standing beside the path holds a red-beribboned, closely swaddled baby in her arms, and as I pass, the bottom wrappings fall. The women then place the babies on their shoulders or on their heads, where they kick their naked legs, smile with pleasure, screech with terror, or occasionally wave. It is a protest and celebration the men threatening them do not even recognize. (*Possessing* 278)

The Olinka women are joined by Tashi's family and friends, African American and African, female and male. Before the soldiers can stop them, they unfurl a banner that proclaims that "RESISTANCE IS THE SECRET OF JOY!" (279). The voice Walker creates is not, by the end of the novel, an individual African woman's voice, but a collective voice in "authentic solidarity" with African people against oppressive practices.

And Alice Walker is not alone in her desire to enact, through litera- ture, a consciously political Pan-Africanist stance. While scholars like Henry Louis Gates, and indeed, Walker herself, claim Zora Neale Hurston as her literary foremother, Walker's creation of African voices in *Possessing* recalls the work of another African American female writer, Lorraine Hansberry. Hansberry, a self-proclaimed feminist, can also be identified as a Pan-African internationalist. Bell hooks points out that "Hansberry was one of the many black artists, writers, thinkers, and intellectuals of her day who were not ashamed to link art and revolution- ary politics, who were not afraid to speak out publicly against white im- perialism in Africa" (*Yearning* 187). But while African American cultural/political workers such as W. E. B. Du Bois, Paul Robeson, and Amiri Baraka have long demonstrated concern with ongoing political struggles in Africa, few contemporary writers have given voice to conti- nental African politics and/or characters in their work. For Hansberry (like Walker), however, this seems to have been a continuing thread through her work.

Hansberry's first play, *A Raisin in the Sun* (1958), introduces the African struggle for independence through the character Assagai, pro- claimed by Hansberry as a Yoruba from Nigeria who is concerned with how best to make his U.S. education work in the service of Nigeria's de- colonization. But her last drama, *Les Blancs* (produced posthumously in 1970 and published in 1972), represents more than simply an African American's imagining of an African character. Rather, African Ameri- cans become a constituency in solidarity with African independence.

Hansberry's own words from a letter responding to a request for her opinion on the seemingly divergent paths, nonviolence versus radicalism, of the U.S. black liberation struggle, resurface in *Les Blancs*. In the United States, "Negroes must concern themselves with every single means of struggle: legal, illegal, passive, active, violent and non-violent. They must harass, debate, petition, give money to court struggles, sit-in, lie-down, strike, boycott, sing hymns, pray on steps—and shoot from their windows when the racists come cruising through their communities" (*To Be Young* 221–22). In *Les Blancs*, Hansberry's protagonist, Tshembe, who has returned to Africa from his current home in England for his father's funeral, is drawn into a discussion about approaches to African independence with white U.S. journalist Charlie Morris. Charlie suggests that Kumalo, who has been representing Zatembe, the fictional setting of Hansberry's play, in the negotiations for indigenous representation in the colonial government, might be enlisted to denounce the "terrorism" employed by the clandestine revolutionaries of the country. Tshembe's reply reiterates Hansberry's position that all forms of resistance must be employed in the struggle against oppression. Tshembe suggests that the minute Kumalo denounced terrorism,

> his bargaining power would vanish. . . . [T]he Europeans have [n]ever been exactly overwhelmed by morality—black *or* white! Or do you think they have suddenly become impressed because Kumalo is *saying* the black man wishes freedom? We have been saying *that* for generations. They only listen now because they are forced to. Take away the violence and who will hear the man of peace? . . . It is the way of the world, hadn't you noticed? (*Les Blancs* 90–91)

In response to the jailing of Kumalo and the murder of Ntali, Tshembe's childhood friend and a leader of the Freedom Army, the last scene of the play finds the mission in flames, the Freedom Army committed to driving out the European colonizers, and Tshembe choosing to remain in Zatembe to join the resistance struggle. Like Walker's *Possessing, Les Blancs* concludes with a call to collective action.

The overt politics of Walker's *Possessing* and Hansberry's *Les Blancs* resound the African American slave narrative, the black arts movement, and a continuing legacy of political engagement of the arts. While bell hooks criticizes *The Color Purple* for appropriating the form of the slave narrative but neglecting its insistence that the "plight of the individual narrator be linked to the oppressed plight of all black people so as to arouse support for organized political effort for social changes" ("Reading and Resistance" 292), *Possessing* revisits the slave narrative form, linking the protagonist's plight to that of all oppressed women. As in the case of the published slave autobiography, extratextual elements of Walker's novel underscore the polemic nature of the narrative, making a direct political appeal to the reader. In a section titled "To the Reader," Walker provides statistics indicating the incidence of the practice of female genital mutilation and refers the reader to nonfiction works that address the practice in Africa and the United States. She also explicates her relationship to the (fictional) narrator, as did the publishers of the original slave narratives. Citing the filming of *The Color Purple* as one incident, Walker relates the tenacious presence of Tashi's spirit. The young Kenyan woman who played Tashi in the film occasions Walker's comment that only in 1982, the year *The Color Purple* was published, did the president of Kenya ban female circumcision following the death of fourteen children. With the realization that such a practice might still be a part of some young African women's realities, Walker returns to Tashi in this latest novel. Because of her heritage of geographic and cultural displacement, Walker claims the entire continent of Africa as her ancestral home, the Olinka as her invented cultural group, and her character Tashi as her sister.

Like Virginia Woolf, who claimed that as a woman she had no country, her country was the world, Alice Walker imagines transnational solidarity on the basis of female identity. But unlike Woolf, who refuses to speak for the "other" in her fiction, Walker gives voice to those whom she calls "family." Colonial domination, the international slave trade, and the resulting displacement have created "hybrid" identities requiring reinvented cultural histories and making more difficult the determination of who qualifies as "other." We can see in her early writings, particularly the essay "My Father's Country Is the Poor," that Walker has long been predisposed to an international perspective on capitalist and colonial exploitation, and subsequently the assault upon female identity by patriarchal domination. In her work, her interest in race and gender assumes international proportions; Walker strategically maneuvers identity across borders and sometimes, as in the character of Tashi, obscures boundaries of identity, collapsing several subjectivities into a single body. It is not only Tashi who is constructed this way but also Lissie in *The Temple of My Familiar*. Lissie stands out among Walker's characters because she seems to defy any understanding of identity that ascribes to narrow nationalism. Lissie's ability to assume multiple identities represents

Walker's capacity to imagine the multiple subjectivities that affirm female selfhood.

The postcolonial, transnationalist impulse of Walker's novels manifests in her critique of the colonial project and global patriarchy, and resides in the indirect discourse of *The Color Purple* (in Nettie's letters to Celie which implicate Christian missionary work in the colonial project). In *The Temple of My Familiar,* it is through the indirect device of Fanny's letters to Suwello that we are introduced to Ola, who moves Walker's critique toward a collective mode of struggle against the neocolonial state and suggests that the cultural worker has a role to play in decolonization. By the time we arrive at the conclusion of *Possessing the Secret of Joy,* Walker's critique is no longer rendered indirectly, but rather in polemic terms. Because Walker's work consistently revisits the international condition of women and of colonially subjugated peoples, the creation of Third World voices, like those of Zedé, Ola, and Tashi, for example, begs the question who can speak for whom. Although we cannot accept these images uncritically, Walker's creation of Third World voices is not a case of appropriation. Walker's creation of Third World voices does not belong to the continuum of "othering." I believe that the voices and images that reside in her novels are the product of genuine solidarity with Third World people struggling against all forms of domination and exploitation. What Walker represents as a politically engaged cultural worker is "joining," a connectedness with oppressed people based upon a shared commitment to resistance. Walker's identity as an African diaspora woman has been too narrowly defined by those who would deny her a voice in matters concerning continental Africans.

NOTES

[1] The practice of female "circumcision," raised by Walker's latest works and addressed later in this chapter, is practiced in its most severe form by some African Muslim cultures and serves as evidence for Walker's observation here.

[2] While I use the terms "female genital mutilation" and "female circumcision" interchangeably here, it must be noted that the two terms are not equivalent. "Female genital mutilation" implies a critical position against the practice and is the term of choice for many political activists and health care workers, in Africa and elsewhere, engaged in the struggle to eradicate the practice. "Circumcision" is less cumbersome linguistically but does not carry the same political connotation. Furthermore, "circumcision" implies a practice that would be equiv-

alent to the male version, involving the removal of the foreskin only. The cutting of the prepuce (hood of the clitoris) could be seen as comparable to the male form. According to Efua Dorkenoo and Scilla Elworthy's *Female Genital Mutilation: Proposals for Change,* this form applies only to a small portion of the millions of women who are affected. Much more common is clitoridectomy, which could be compared to the excision of the penis. This form is sometimes accompanied by removal (to varying extent) of parts of the labia minora and labia majora, and pulling closed the resulting wound, leaving only a small opening for the passage of urine and menstrual blood. It is this form, known as infibulation, which Walker portrays in *Possessing the Secret of Joy.*

[3]This surgical procedure was advertised as a way to make the clitoris more available (by excising the hood or prepuce) to direct stimulation by the penis, with the obvious though unstated heterosexist assumption that vaginal intercourse (à la Freud) is the preferable form of sexual practice. When confronted by several of his female patients who complained of pain during intercourse, Burt admitted that the surgery was actually designed to increase *male* pleasure by tightening the vaginal opening.

[4]According to *The Hosken Report,* the practice occurs most frequently in the heavily Islamic countries of eastern Africa.

[5]The United Nations Convention to Eliminate All Forms of Discrimination Against Women and the Children's Rights Convention address the health and well-being of women and children generally, and specifically oppose the practice of female genital mutilation.

[6]In 1990, the African Charter of the Rights and Welfare of the Child was adopted by the Organization of African Unity, promoting gender equality among children and requiring all governments that sign the charter to "take all appropriate measures to eliminate harmful social and cultural practices affecting children, including practices that are discriminatory on the basis of sex" (Toubia 45).

[7]Toubia notes that many countries in which FGM is or has been practiced now have national laws or official policies against the practice. For example, Kenya banned FGM in 1990; in 1991, an official from the Ivory Coast claimed to the United Nations that the practice could be prosecuted under the existing criminal code; and in 1994 Ghana passed a law that explicitly prohibits FGM.

Epilogue

The assumption of this study that the ideas of transnational feminism can be appropriately applied to literary texts raises once again the "politics vs. aesthetics" argument that has plagued the production and critical reception of Third World literatures. At the heart of my project lies the question: What is the responsibility of aesthetic expression to the plight of the oppressed? Art has never been divorced from politics; W. E. B. DuBois asserts that

> all Art is propaganda and ever must be, despite the wailing of the purists. I stand in utter shamelessness and say that whatever art I have for writing has been used always for propaganda for gaining the right of black folk to love and enjoy. I do not care a damn for any art that is not used for propaganda. But I do care when propaganda is confined to one side while the other is stripped and silent. (296)

Houston Baker agrees: "The negative propaganda on one side of the 'veil' described by DuBois should occasion a resistant form of proselytizing" (Baker 51). To consider art an agency of societal change is to accept certain *a priori* assumptions, one being that a critical approach to it must be socially oriented (Baker 51).

The application of transnational feminist ideas to the literary texts under study in this project exemplifies the kind of socially oriented critical approach called for in the interpretation of these texts. A transnational feminist approach to the study of literature affirms the voices of the once silenced and marginalized subjects erased by master narratives

and constricted by narrow forms of nationalism. Grewal and Kaplan call
for a thorough critique of modernity and its institutions including national identity. "The need to free feminism from nationalist discourses is
clear. Yet feminism is implicated in nationalism as well as in its counter
discourses" (*Scattered Hegemonies* 22). My approach reads the feminist,
postmodern explorations of subject construction generated in artistic
production from multiple peripheries—newly independent states currently engaged in decolonization and postcolonial diasporas, for example—as radical political acts.

Cultural workers such as Alice Walker may be marginalized as subjects of internal colonization, yet Walker's achieved class position in a
First World diaspora affords her the opportunity to bring available tech-
nology to bear upon the issue of female genital mutilation in solidarity
with continental African women. Her novel *Possessing the Secret of Joy,*
her documentary film *Warrior Marks,* and the companion personal journal function as a systematic, transnational attack on this practice as one
in a network of practices which oppress women globally. While I find
some aspects of the manner in which Walker executes her film critique
troublesome, the three works together exemplify a kind of coalition politics informed by transnational feminism.

Possessing the Secret of Joy, analyzed in chapter 4 of this study,
imagines an extreme form of resistance to the practice by an African
character with a level of popular support among her countrywomen. This
kind of support might be dismissed as wishful thinking on the part of a
sympathetic US author or as simply a literary example of the influence of
Western feminism on an African character who spends much of her adult
life in the US. The film and journal work against both assumptions, revealing through interviews with health care workers and activists on the
continent that while African women may utilize the various forms
through which information flows globally, they have not needed Western
feminists to lead them in organizing against cultural practices that endan-
ger their own lives.

The film needs to be interpreted through the self-reflexive stance of
the journal co-authored by Walker and the filmmaker for this project,
Pratibha Parmar. The journal offers more than a day-to-day, first person
account of their filmmaking process. It also provides a structure for foregrounding the introspection of these two cultural workers as they approach this project and consider the troubling problem of speaking for
others. Walker considers the practice of female genital mutilation in light
of the many forms of mutilation and self-mutilation in which Western

women take part. Parmar, born in Kenya of South Asian descent, recalls her earlier film on the practice of *sati,* the Hindu cultural practice that dictates that a widow must throw herself on her husband's funeral pyre. Parmar, like Walker, approaches the subject of *Warrier Marks* as one who has addressed oppressive cultural practices on a local level and moved to make transnational connections. The journal serves Walker and Parmar as an opportunity to demonstrate a transnational feminist praxis. The journal form allows them to more successfully accomplish what is often difficult in academic work and I have found the hardest part of my project—keeping my own politics visible and investigating the ways in which I may stand in collusion with the forces of oppression. This is crucial in the case of a film like *Warrior Marks* which has the potential to reach a wide audience and risks exoticizing African women in the process. The questions of how to show the film so that it may be informed by the journal and of who is the intended audience for such a performance might be fruitful sites for articulating another kind of transnational feminist practice.

It seems equally crucial for a critic who claims that the analysis of literature is a political act to examine the material conditions that give rise to the academic consumption of literature. A thorough examination of that is beyond the scope of this epilogue, but I would like to suggest that academia can and should be an arena for transnational feminist praxis. Curricular issues, syllabus construction, teaching methods, and evaluation procedures might provide fruitful sites of struggle. As I have attempted to demonstrate in this project, examining the material conditions of literary production, along with producing literary analysis which takes into account the social and critical contexts of colonial, postcolonial, and neocolonial settings may be ways to enact transnational feminism in the classroom.

Bibliography

Abel, Elizabeth. "Black Writing, White Reading: Race and the Politics of Feminist Interpretation." *Critical Inquiry* 19 (1993): 470–98.

Achebe, Chinua. "The African Writer and the English Language." *Morning Yet on Creation Day*. New York: Anchor, 1975. 91–102. Rpt. in *Colonial Discourse and Post-Colonial Theory: A Reader*. Ed. Patrick Williams and Laura Chrisman. New York: Columbia UP, 1994. 428–34.

———. "An Image of Africa: Racism in Conrad's *Heart of Darkness*." 1975. Rpt. in *Hopes and Impediments: Selected Essays*. New York: Doubleday, 1989. 1–20.

———. *No Longer at Ease*. New York: Fawcett, 1960.

———. *Things Fall Apart*. New York: Fawcett, 1959.

Ahmad, Aijaz. *In Theory: Nations, Classes, Literatures*. London: Verso, 1992.

Albrinck, Meg. "Voyaging between Acts of Imperialism: Framing Virginia Woolf's Struggle with the Binaries of Empire." Unpublished essay, 1995.

Alcoff, Linda. "The Problem of Speaking for Others." *Cultural Critique* 20 (1991–92): 5–32.

Anand, Mulk Raj. *Untouchable*. 1935. London: Penguin, 1986.

Anderson, Benedict. *Imagined Communities*. 1983. London: Verso, 1991.

Anzaldúa, Gloria. *Borderlands/La Frontera: The New Mestiza*. San Francisco: Aunt Lute, 1987.

Appadurai, Arjun. "Disjuncture and Difference in the Global Cultural Economy." *Public Culture* 2.2 (1990): 1–24. Rpt. in *Colonial Discourse and Post-Colonial Theory: A Reader*. Ed. Patrick Williams and Laura Chrisman. New York: Columbia UP, 1994. 324–49.

Ashcroft, Bill, Gareth Griffiths, and Helen Tiffin. *The Empire Writes Back: Theory and Practice in Post-Colonial Literatures*. 1989. London: Routledge, 1993.

Athey, Stephanie, and Daniel Cooper Alarcón. "*Oroonoko*'s Gendered Economies of Honor/Horror: Reframing Colonial Discourse Studies in the Americas." *American Literature* 65.3 (1993): 415–43.

Bâ, Mariama. *So Long a Letter*. Trans. Modupé Bodé-Thomas. 1981. Oxford: Heinemann, 1989.

Baker, Houston A. *Afro-American Poetics: Revisions of Harlem and the Black Aesthetic*. Madison: U of Wisconsin P, 1988.

Bakhtin, M. M. "Discourse in the Novel." *The Dialogic Imagination*. Trans. Caryl Emerson and Michael Holquist. Austin: U of Texas P, 1981.

Baldwin, James. *Another Country*. 1960. New York: Dell, 1963.

———. "Everybody's Protest Novel." *Notes of a Native Son*. 1955. Boston: Beacon, 1964.

———. *Giovanni's Room*. 1956. New York: Dell, 1988.

Barksdale, Richard, and Kenneth Kinnamon. "The Present Generation: Since 1945." *Black Writers of America: A Comprehensive Anthology*. Ed. Richard Barksdale and Keneth Kinnamon. New York: Macmillan, 1972. 643–889.

Barnes, Fiona Ruthven. "Explorations in Geography, Gender and Genre: Decolonizing Women's Novels of Development." Diss. U of Wisconsin–Madison, 1993.

Bayley, John. "Diminishment of Consciousness: A Paradox in the Art of Virginia Woolf." *Virginia Woolf: A Centenary Perspective*. Ed. Eric Warner. London: Macmillan, 1984. 69–82.

Bazin, Nancy Topping. "Weight of Custom, Signs of Change: Feminism in the Literature of African Women." *World Literature Written in English* 25.2 (1985): 183–97.

Beer, Gilliam. "Virginia Woolf and Pre-History." *Virginia Woolf: A Centenary Perspective*. Ed. Eric Warner. London: Macmillan, 1984. 99–123.

Bell, Quentin. *Virginia Woolf: A Biography*. New York: Harcourt Brace Jovanovich, 1972.

Benjamin, Walter. "The Work of Art in the Age of Mechanical Reproduction." *Illuminations*. Ed. Hannah Arendt. Trans. Harry Zohn. New York: Harcourt, Brace & World, 1968. 219–53.

Berlant, Lauren. "Race, Gender, and Nation in *The Color Purple*." *Critical Inquiry* 14.4 (1988): 831–59.

Bhabha, Homi. *The Location of Culture*. London: Routledge, 1994.

Bloom, Harold. *The Western Canon*. New York: Harcourt Brace & Co., 1994.

Bowen, Barbara E. "Writing Caliban: Anticolonial Appropriations of *The Tempest*." *Current Writing: Text and Reception in Southern Africa* 5.2 (1993): 80–99.

Boyd, Melba Joyce. "The Politics of Cherokee Spirituality in Alice Walker's *Meridian.*" *Working Papers: The Black Woman, Challenges and Prospects for the Future*. Proc. of a conference, May 3–5, 1988. Columbus: Ohio State Black Studies Extension Center, 1991. 13–28.

Brydon, Diana. "Re-writing *The Tempest.*" *World Literature Written in English* 23.1 (1984): 75–88.

Busia, Abena P. A. "Silencing Sycorax: On African Colonial Discourse and the Unvoiced Female." *Cultural Critique* 14 (1990): 81–104.

Carmichael, Stokely, and Charles V. Hamilton. *Black Power: The Politics of Liberation in America*. New York: Random House, 1967.

Carter, Steven R. "Colonialism and Culture in Lorraine Hansberry's *Les Blancs.*" *MELUS* 15.1 (1988): 27–46.

Césaire, Aimé. *Discourse on Colonialism*. 1955. Trans. Joan Pinkham. New York: Monthly Review P, 1972.

Cheatwood, K. T. H. Rev. of *Horses Make a Landscape Look More Beautiful,* by Alice Walker. *Virginia News Leader* Winter 1984.

Chinweizu et al. *The West and the Rest of Us*. Lagos: Pero, 1987.

Christian, Barbara. "The Race for Theory." *Making Face, Making Soul:* Haciendo Caras: *Creative and Critical Perspectives by Women of Color*. Ed. Gloria Anzaldúa. San Francisco: Aunt Lute, 1990. 335–45.

Christie, Sarah, Geoffrey Hutchings, and Don Maclennan. *Perspectives on South African Fiction*. Johannesburg: Ad. Donker, 1980.

Coetzee, J. M. *Doubling the Point*. Ed. David Attwell. Cambridge: Harvard UP, 1992.

———. *Waiting for the Barbarians*. New York: Penguin, 1980.

Conrad, Joseph. *Heart of Darkness*. 1899. Rpt. in *Heart of Darkness: A Case Study in Contemporary Criticism*. Ed. Ross Murfin. New York: St. Martin's, 1989. 17–94.

Davis, Angela Y. *Women, Culture, and Politics*. New York: Random House, 1989.

Decker, Jeffrey Louis. "Terrorism (Un)Veiled: Frantz Fanon and the Women of Algiers." *Cultural Critique* (1990–91): 177–95.

Dodd, Josephine. "The South African Literary Establishment and the Textual Production of 'Woman': J. M. Coetzee and Lewis Nkosi." *Current Writing* 2 (1990): 117–29.

Dorkenoo, Efua, and Scilla Elworthy. *Female Circumcision, Excision, and Infibulation*. 1983. Rpt. as *Female Genital Mutilation: Proposals for Change*. Manchester: Manchester Free P, 1994.

Du Bois, W. E. B. "Criteria of Negro Art." *Crisis* 32 (1926): 296.

Eagleton, Terry, Frederic Jameson, and Edward W. Said. *Nationalism, Colonialism, and Literature*. Minneapolis: U of Minnesota P, 1990.

El Saadawi, Nawal. *The Hidden Face of Eve: Women in the Arab World*. Trans. Sherif Hetata. Boston: Beacon, 1982.

Emecheta, Buchi. *The Joys of Motherhood*. New York: George Braziller, 1979.

Fanon, Frantz. *Black Skin, White Masks*. Trans. Charles Lam Markmann. New York: Grove, 1967.

————. *The Wretched of the Earth*. New York: Grove, 1963.

February, V. A. *Mind Your Colour: The "Coloured" Stereotype in South African Literature*. London: Kegan Paul, 1981.

Forster, E. M. *A Passage to India*. 1924. New York: Harcourt, Brace & World, 1952.

Foucault, Michel. "What Is an Author?" *The Foucault Reader*. Ed. Paul Rabinow. New York: Pantheon, 1984. 101–20.

Fuss, Diana. "The 'Risk' of Essence." *Essentially Speaking: Feminism, Nature, and Difference*. New York: Routledge, 1989. 1–21.

Gates, Henry Louis, Jr. *The Signifying Monkey: A Theory of African-American Literary Criticism*. New York: Oxford UP, 1988.

————. "Writing 'Race' and the Difference It Makes." *"Race," Writing, and Difference*. Ed. Henry Louis Gates, Jr. Chicago: U of Chicago P, 1986. 1–20.

Gordimer, Nadine. *Burger's Daughter*. London: Penguin, 1979.

————. *July's People*. New York, Penguin, 1981.

————. *My Son's Story*. New York: Penguin, 1990.

Grewal, Inderpal, and Caren Kaplan, eds. *Scattered Hegemonies: Postmodernity and Transnational Feminist Practices*. Inderpal Caren. Minneapolis: U of Minnesota P, 1994.

Griffiths, Trevor R. " 'This Island's Mine': Caliban and Colonialism." *Yearbook of English Studies* 13 (1983): 159–80.

Gugelberger, Georg M. "Marxist Literary Debates and Their Continuity in African Literary Criticism." *Marxism and African Literature*. Ed. Georg M. Gugelberger. London: James Currey, 1985. 1–20.

Hall, Stuart. "Cultural Identity and Diaspora." *Identity: Community, Culture, Difference*. Ed. J. Rutherford. London: Lawrence & Wishart, 1990. 222–37. Rpt. in *Colonial Discourse and Post-Colonial Theory: A Reader*. Ed. Patrick Williams and Laura Chrisman. New York: Columbia UP, 1994. 392–403.

Hamner, Robert. "Colony, Nationhood, and Beyond: Third World Writers and Critics Content with Joseph Conrad." *World Literature Written in English* 23.1 (1984): 108–16.

Hansberry, Lorraine. *Les Blancs: The Collected Last Plays*. Ed. Robert Nemiroff. New York: Random House, 1994.

————. *A Raisin in the Sun*. 1958. New York: Signet, 1988.

————. *To Be Young, Gifted, and Black: Lorraine Hansberry in Her Own Words.* Adapted by Robert Nemiroff. New York: Signet, 1970.

Harper, Howard. *Between Language and Silence: The Novels of Virginia Woolf.* Baton Rouge: Louisiana State UP, 1982. 1–56.

Harris, Trudier. "From Victimization to Free Enterprise: Alice Walker's *The Color Purple.*" *Studies in American Fiction* 14.1 (1986): 1–17.

————. "On *The Color Purple,* Stereotypes, and Silence." *Black American Literature Forum* 18.4 (1984): 155–61.

Harris, Wilson. "The Frontier on Which *Heart of Darkness* Stands." *Research in African Literatures* 12.1 (1981): 86–93.

Head, Bessie. *Maru.* 1971. Oxford: Heinemann, 1988.

————. *A Question of Power.* 1974. London: Heinemann, 1987.

————. *When Rain Clouds Gather.* 1969. London: Heinemann, 1987.

Herzog, Anne. "Adrienne Rich and the Discourse of Decolonization." *The Centennial Review* 33.3 (1989): 257–77.

hooks, bell. *Black Looks: Race and Representation.* Boston: South End, 1992.

————. "Reading and Resistance: *The Color Purple.*" *Alice Walker: Critical Perspectives Past and Present.* Ed. Henry Louis Gates, Jr., and K. A. Appiah. New York: Amistad, 1993. 284–95.

————. *Yearning: Race, Gender, and Cultural Politics.* Boston: South End, 1990.

Hosken, Fran P. *The Hosken Report: Genital and Sexual Mutilation of Females.* 4th rev. Lexington, MA: WIN News, 1993.

Irigaray, Luce. "Women on the Market." *This Sex Which Is Not One.* Trans. Catherine Porter. Ithaca: Cornell UP, 1985. 170–91.

Jameson, Fredric. "Third-World Literature in the Era of Multinational Capitalism." *Social Text* 15 (1986): 65–88.

Jeyifo, Biodun. *The Truthful Lie: Essays in a Sociology of African Drama.* London: New Beacon, 1985.

Johnson, Joyce. "Metaphor, Myth, and Meaning in Bessie Head's *A Question of Power.*" *World Literature Written in English* 25.2 (1985): 198–211.

Joplin, Patricia Klindienst. "The Authority of Illusion: Feminism and Facism in Virginia Woolf's *Between the Acts.*" *Virginia Woolf: A Collection of Critical Essays.* Ed. Margaret Homans. Englewood Cliffs: Prentice-Hall, 1993. 210–26.

Juneja, Om P. "The Purple Colour of Walker Women: Their Journey from Slavery to Liberation." *The Literary Criterion* 25.3 (1990): 66–76.

King, Bruce. "Introduction: A Changing Face." *The Later Fiction of Nadine Gordimer.* Ed. B. King. New York: St. Martin's, 1993. 1–20.

Kipling, Rudyard. *Kim.* 1901. London: Penguin, 1989.

Lamming, George. *The Pleasures of Exile.* 1960. Ann Arbor: U of Michigan P, 1992.

Laurence, Patrica Ondek. *The Reading of Silence: Virginia Woolf in the English Tradition.* Stanford: Stanford UP, 1991.

Lazarus, Neil. *Resistance in Postcolonial African Fiction.* New Haven: Yale UP, 1990.

Le Guin, Ursula K. Rev. of *The Temple of My Familiar. Alice Walker: Critical Perspectives.* New York: Amistad, 1993. 22–23.

Lindfors, Bernth. "Coming to Terms with the Apocalypse: Recent South African Fiction." *A Sense of Place: Essays in Post-Colonial Literatures.* Ed. Britta Olinder. Göteborg: Gothenburg U: 1984. 196–203.

Lockett, Cecily. "Feminism(s) and Writing in English in South Africa." *Current Writing* 2 (1990): 1–21.

Lorde, Audre. *Sister Outsider.* Trumansburg, NY: Crossing, 1984.

Lubiano, Wahneema. "Shuckin' Off the African-American Native Other: What's 'Po-Mo' Got to Do with It?" *Cultural Critique* 18 (1991): 149–85.

Lugones, María. "Playfulness, 'World'-Travelling, and Loving Perception." *Making Face, Making Soul/Hacienda Caras: Creative and Critical Perspectives by Women of Color.* Ed. Gloria Anzaldúa. San Francisco: Aunt Lute, 1990. 390–402.

Lynch, Eve. "The Cook, the Nurse, the Maid, and the Mother: Woolf's Working Women." *Virginia Woolf: Themes and Variations.* Ed. Vara Neverow-Turk and Mark Hussey. New York: Pace UP, 1991. 68–75.

Macaulay, Lord Thomas Babington. "Minute on Indian Education." *Selected Writings.* Ed. John Clive and Thomas Pinney. Chicago: U of Chicago P, 1972. 237–51.

MacKenzie, Craig, ed. *Bessie Head, a Woman Alone: Autobiographical Writings.* Oxford: Heinemann, 1990.

Maqagi, Sisi. "Who Theorises?" *Current Writing* 2 (1990): 22–25.

Marais, Sue. "Ivan Vladislavic's Re-vision of the South African Story Cycle." *Current Writing* 4 (1992): 41–55.

Marcus, Jane. "Britiannia Rules *The Waves.*" *Decolonizing Tradition: New Views of 20th Century "British" Literary Canons.* Ed. Karen R. Lawrence. Urbana: U of Illinois P, 1992. 136–62.

Martin, Richard G. "Narrative, History, Ideology: A Study of *Waiting for the Barbarians and Burger's Daughter.*" *ARIEL (A Review of International English Literature)* 17.3 (1986): 3–21.

McClintock, Anne. "The Angel of Progress: Pitfalls of the Term 'Post-Colonialism.' " *Social Text* 31/32 (1992): 84–98.

Miller, Nancy K. *Subject to Change*. New York: Columbia UP, 1988.

Minh-ha, Trinh T. "Not You/Like You: Post-Colonial Women and the Interlocking Questions of Identity and Difference." *Making Face, Making Soul:* Haciendo Caras: *Creative and Critical Perspectives by Women of Color*. Ed. Gloria Anzaldúa. San Francisco: Aunt Lute, 1990. 371–75.

Mohanty, Chandra Talpade. "Under Western Eyes: Feminist Scholarship and Colonial Discourse." *Third World Womena nd the Politics of Feminism*. Ed. C. Mohanty et al. Bloomington: Indiana UP, 1991. 51–80.

Mohanty, Satya P. "Drawing the Color Line: Kipling and the Culture of Colonial Rule." *The Bounds of Race: Perspectives on Hegemony and Resistance*. Ed. Dominick LaCapra. Ithaca: Cornell UP, 1991. 311–43.

Moore, Madeline. *The Short Season between Two Silences*. Boston: Allen & Unwin, 1984.

Morrison, Toni. *Playing in the Dark: Whiteness and the Literary Imagination*. New York: Vintage, 1990.

———. "The Site of Memory." *Out There: Marginalization and Contemporary Cultures*. New York: MIT P, 1990. 299–305.

———. "Unspeakable Things Unspoken: The Afro-American Presence in American Literature." *Michigan Quarterly Review* 28.1 (1989): 1–34.

Mphande, Lupenga, and Ikechukwu Okafor-Newsum. "Popular Music, Appropriation, and the Circular Culture of Labor Migration in Southern Africa: The Case of South Africa and Malawi." U of Pittsburgh. Black Popular Culture Conference. Pittsburgh, April 6–8, 1994.

Mudimbe, V. Y. *The Invention of Africa: Gnosis, Philosophy, and the Order of Knowledge*. Bloomington: Indiana UP, 1988.

Newsum, H. E. *Class, Language, and Education: Sociolinguistics in an African Situation*. Trenton: Africa World, 1990.

Nkosi, Lewis. *Mating Birds*. New York: St. Martin's, 1986.

———. *The Rhythm of Violence*. London: Oxford UP, 1964.

———. "Southern Africa: Protest and Commitment." *Tasks and Masks: Themes and Styles of African Literature*. Essex: Longman, 1981. 76–106.

Nussbaum, Felicity A. "Autobiographical Spaces and the Postcolonial Predicament." *Current Writing* 3 (1991): 24–30.

Ngũgĩ wa Thiong'o. *Decolonizing the Mind: The Politics of Language in African Literature*. London: James Currey, 1986.

Olaussen, Maria. "Jean Rhys's Construction of Blackness as Escape from White Femininity in *Wide Sargasso Sea*." *ARIEL (A Review of International English Literature)* 24.2 (1993): 65–82.

Oliver, Roland, and J. D. Fage. *A Short History of Africa*. Middlesex: Penguin, 1962.

Onoge, Omafume F. "The Crisis of Consciousness in Modern African Literature. *Marxism and African Literature*. London: James Currey, 1985. 21–49.

Ravenscroft, Arthur. "The Novels of Bessie Head." *Aspects of South African Literature*. Ed. Christopher Heywood. London: Heinemann, 1976. 174–86.

Reagon, Bernice Johnson. "Coalition Politics: Turning the Century." *Home Girls: A Black Feminist Anthology*. Ed. Barbara Smith. New York: Kitchen Table: Women of Color P, 1983. 356–69.

Reuck, Jenny de. "Writing Feminism/Theoretical Inscriptions in South Africa." *Current Writing* 2 (1990): 30–43.

Rich, Adrienne. "Notes toward a Politics of Location (1984)." *Blood, Bread, and Poetry: Selected Prose: 1979–1985*. New York: Norton, 1986. 210–31.

Riemenschneider, Dieter. "Ngũgĩ wa Thiong'o and the Question of Language and Literature in Kenya." *World Literature Written in English* 24.1 (1984): 78–86.

Rubin, Gayle. "The Traffic in Women: Notes on the 'Political Economy' of Sex." *Toward an Anthropology of Women*. Ed. Rayna R. Reiter. New York: Monthly Review P, 1975. 157–210.

Ryan, Pamela. "The Future of South African Feminism." *Current Writing* 2 (1990): 26–29.

Said, Edward W. *Culture and Imperialism*. New York: Vintage, 1993.

———. *Orientalism*. New York: Vintage, 1978.

Sandoval, Chela. "U.S. Third World Feminism: The Theory and Method of Oppositional Consciousness in the Postmodern World." *Genders* 10 (1991): 1–24.

Schalkwyk, David. "The Authority of Experience or the Tyranny of Discourse: An Inescapable Impasse?" *Current Writing* 2 (1990): 45–62.

Schneider, Karen. "Of Two Minds: Woolf, the War, and *Between the Acts*." *Journal of Modern Literature* 16.1 (1989): 93–112.

Schwerdt, Dianne. "Deconstructing Cultural Imperialism: African Literature and the Politics of Language." *Southern Review* 24 (1991): 57–68.

Shakespeare, William. *Much Ado About Nothing*. Textual ed. G. Blakemore Evans. Riverside ed. Boston: Houghton Mifflin, 1974. 327–64.

———. *The Tempest. The Riverside Shakespeare*. Ed. G. Blakemore Evans. Boston: Houghton Mifflin, 1974. 1606–38.

Sharpe, Jenny. "The Unspeakable Limits of Rape: Colonial Violence and Counter-Insurgency." *Genders* 10 (1991): 25–46. Rpt. in *Colonial Discourse and Post-Colonial Literature: A Reader*. Ed. Patrick Williams and Laura Chrisman. New York: Columbia UP, 1994. 221–43.

Shohat, Ella. "Notes on the 'Post-Colonial.' " *Social Text* 31/32 (1992): 99–113.

Sicherman, Carol. "Zoë Wicomb's *You Can't Get Lost in Cape Town:* The Narrator's Identity." *Black/White Writing: Essays on South African Literature.* Ed. Pauline Fletcher. Lewisburg: Bucknell UP, 1993. 111–22.

Skura, Meredith Anne. "Discourse and the Individual: The Case of Colonialism in *The Tempest.*" *Shakespeare Quarterly* 40.1 (1989): 42–69.

Spivak, Gayatri Chakravorty. "Can the Subaltern Speak?" *Marxism and the Interpretation of Culture.* Ed. C. Nelson and L. Grossberg. Urbana: U of Illinois P, 1988. 271–313.

———. "Introduction." *Subaltern Studies: Deconstructing Historiography.* Ed. Ranajit Guha and Gayatri Spivak. London: Oxford UP, 1988. 3–35.

———. "The Problem of Cultural Self-Representation." *The Post-Colonial Critic: Interviews, Strategies, Dialogues.* Ed. Sarah Harasym. New York: Routledge, 1990. 50–58.

———. *Thinking Academic Freedom in Gendered Post-Coloniality.* Cape Town: U of Cape Town, 1992.

———. "Three Women's Texts and a Critique of Imperialism." *"Race," Writing, and Difference.* Chicago: U of Chicago P, 1986. 262–80.

Suleri, Sara. "Woman Skin Deep: Feminism and the Postcolonial Condition." *Critical Inquiry* 18 (1992): 756–69. Rpt. in *Colonial Discourse and Post-Colonial Literature: A Reader.* Ed. Patrick Williams and Laura Chrisman. New York: Columbia UP, 1994. 244–56.

Taylor, Elizabeth, "Tradition and the Woman Writer in Southern Africa, or How to Enjoy the River without Carrying the Water Drums." *Black/White Writing: Essays on South African Literature.* Ed. Pauline Fletcher. Lewisburg: Bucknell UP, 1993. 99–110.

Tlali, Miriam. *Muriel at Metropolitan.* 1979. London: Longman, 1987.

———. *Soweto Stories.* London: Pandora, 1989.

Toubia, Nahid. *Female Genital Mutilation: A Call for Global Action.* New York: Rainbọ, 1995.

Transue, Pamela J. *Virginia Woolf and the Politics of Style.* Albany: SUNY P, 1986. 1–34.

Traub, Valerie. "The (In)Significance of 'Lesbian' Desire in Early Modern England." *Erotic Politics: Desire on the Renaissance Stage.* Ed. Susan Zimmerman. New York: Routledge, 1992. 150–69.

Viola, André. "Zoë Wicomb's *You Can't Get Lost in Cape Town:* A Portrait of the Artist as a Young Coloured Girl." *Short Fiction in the New Literatures in English.* Ed. J. Bardolph. *Proceedings of the Nice Conference of the European Association for Commonwealth Literature and Language Studies.* Nice: U of Nice, 1988. 231–36.

Visel, Robin. "Othering the Self: Nadine Gordimer's Colonial Heroines." *ARIEL (A Review of International English Literature)* 19.4 (1988): 33–42.

Walker, Alice. *The Color Purple.* 1982. New York: Washington Square, 1983.

———. "Diary of an African Nun." *In Love and Trouble.* New York: Harcourt Brace Jovanovich, 1973, 113–228. Originally published in *Freedomways* 8.3 (1968): 226–29.

———. *Meridian.* 1976. New York: Pocket Books, 1977.

———. "My Father's Country Is the Poor." 1977. *In Search of Our Mother's Gardens.* Harcourt Brace Jovanovich, 1984. 199–222.

———. *Possessing the Secret of Joy.* New York: Harcourt Brace Jovanovich, 1992.

———. "To the Editors of *Ms.* Magazine." *In Search of Our Mothers' Gardens.* San Diego: Harcourt Brace Jovanovich, 1984, 347–54.

———. *The Temple of My Familiar.* New York: Harcourt Brace Jovanovich, 1989.

Walker, Alice, and Pratibha Parmar. *Warrior Marks: Female Genital Mutilation and the Sexual Blinding of Women.* London: Random House, 1993.

Wall, Wendy. "Lettered Bodies and Corporeal Texts in *The Color Purple.*" *Studies in American Fiction* 16.1 (1988): 83–97.

Watson, Stephen. "Colonialism and the Novels of J. M. Coetzee." *Research in African Literatures* 17.3 (1986): 370–92.

Watts, Cedric. " 'A Bloody Racist': About Achebe's View of Conrad." *Yearbook of English Studies* 13 (1983): 196–209.

Wicomb, Zoë. "An Author's Agenda." *Critical Fictions.* Ed. Philomena Mariani. Seattle: Bay, 1991. 13–16.

———. "Culture Beyond Color? A South African Dilemma." *Transition* 60 (1993): 27–32.

———. "Nation, Race, and Ethnicity: Beyond the Legacy of Victims." *Current Writing* 4 (1992): 15–20.

———. "Postcoloniality and Postmodernity: The Case of the Coloured in South Africa." Unpublished essay, 1995.

———. "To Hear the Variety of Discourses." *Current Writing* 2 (1990): 35–44.

———. "Tracing the Path from National to Official Culture." *Critical Fictions.* Ed. Philomena Mariani. Seattle: Bay, 1991. 242–50.

———. *You Can't Get Lost in Cape Town.* New York: Pantheon, 1987.

Wideman, John Edgar. *Philadelphia Fire.* 1990. New York: Vintage, 1991.

Wisker, Gina. " 'Disremembered and Unaccounted For': Reading Toni Morrison's *Beloved* and Alice Walker's *The Temple of My Familiar.*" *Black Women's Writing.* Ed. Gina Wisker. New York: St. Martin's, 1993. 78–95.

Wolff, Cynthia Griffin. " 'Margaret Garner': A Cincinnati Story." *Discovering Difference: Contemporary Essays in American Culture*. Ed. Christoph K. Lohmann. Bloomington: Indiana UP, 1993. 105–22.

Woolf, Virginia. *Between the Acts*. 1941. New York: Harcourt Brace Jovanovich, 1969.

———. *Mrs. Dalloway*. 1925. New York: Harcourt Brace Jovanovich, n.d.

———. *A Room of One's Own*. 1929. New York: Harcourt Brace Jovanovich, n.d.

———. *Three Guineas*. New York: Harcourt Brace & Co., 1938.

———. *To the Lighthouse*. 1927. San Diego: Harcourt Brace Jovanovich, 1989.

———. *The Voyage Out*. 1920. San Diego: Harcourt Brace Jovanovich, n.d.

———. *The Waves*. 1931. San Diego: Harcourt Brace Jovanovich, n.d.

Wright, Richard. *Native Son*. 1940. New York: Harper & Row, 1966.

Zabus, Chantal. "A Calibanic Tempest in Anglophone and Francophone New World Writing." *Canadian Literature* 104 (1985): 35–50.

Index